Praise for Rhonda Jones and *The Christian Meditation Journal*

The journal is great. One thing to realize your journal is a journey in and of itself. Building a Foundation really challenges you to think and examine your life and where you are actually when it comes to your relationship with God. This journal is life-changing."

- Natalie Johnson Lee

Rhonda your book is helping me beyond measure. We have to constantly put on the FULL ARMOR of GOD! I am making a "date with God" every day and it is helping me to stay focused on HIM and not get thrown back and forth emotionally, and in and out of dark places like doubt and despair."

- Peggy Edgerly

OH MY LORD! IT'S AMAZING! In a time where social media and technology have captured the minds of not just unbelievers, but believers also, this is crucial for turning our minds back to God. No one desires to or has the time to meditate on the presence of God and His Word. Success and worldly desires have taken our minds hostage. I believe we're living in a culture that is hungry and thirsty for what you are doing!

-Tony Westbrook, Minister

the christian meditation journal

Rhonda Jones

ISBN-13: 9780964100800-1-7

Paperback: Product Dimensions: 7 x 10 x 0.5 inches

Serenity Enterprises Publications
8250 Calvine Road C185
Sacramento, CA. 95828

Disclaimer
The information in this guide should be considered as general information only and should not be used to diagnose medical conditions. This guide is sold with the understanding that neither the publisher nor author is engaged in rendering medical advice. The author and publisher shall in no event be held liable for any loss or damages, including but not limited to special, incidental, consequential, or other damages. On any spiritual, mental, nutrition, detox, or exercise plan, individual weight loss results will vary. Your results will vary based on many factors.

Please see your health care provider for diagnosis and treatment of any medical concerns, and before implementing any nutrition, exercise or other lifestyle changes.

God Getaway Christian Meditation Retreats
Additional Christian Meditation Courses & Groups
CDs, Downloads, Listening Library, and Bundles
Videos & Articles
Unplug Personal Retreat Kits

Coming Soon! *Design Your Day, Design Your Life Manifesting Journal*

Join the Christian Meditator Mailing Lists!

https://thechristianmeditator.com
http://www.thechristianmeditationjournal.com
https://godgetaways.com

"You will seek me and find me when you search for me with all your heart."

Jeremiah 29:13

"Draw nigh to God and he will draw nigh to you."

James 4:8

Table of Contents

Preface 9

Introduction 17

BUILDING A SPIRITUAL FOUNDATION **21**

Who's Doing the Work? 21

Are You Ready to Make an Appointment? 25

Seeking Creation vs. the Creator? 29

Getting Centered in the Son 35

Manna for Today...39

But Why One Hour? Let's Look at Scripture! 43

Pursuing God # 1 47

Pursuing God # 2 53

Put on the Full Armor of God 59

What Can I Expect from Pursuing God? 63

Why Meditate? 67

Living in Alignment with God & Your Purpose # 1 71

13 Steps to Living in Alignment with God & Your Purpose # 2.................77

THE BASICS **87**

Getting Started 87

Set an Appointment with God..91

Preparing to Meditate 93

Invite God into Your Meditation Practice 97

Let's Meditate 101

Observing Your Thoughts 105

Am I Meditating Correctly? 109

What You Can Feel You Can Heal 113

Where is God in All this Meditating? 117

Scripture and Passage Meditation..121

Daily Self-Care Routine...125

Checking In & Taking Inventory 129

Set an Intention 133

Closing Prayer 135

MOVING BEYOND THE BASICS **139**

Praise and Worship 141

DAILY DEVOTIONAL READING 145

MEDITATE ON GOD'S WORD 149

PRAYER & INTERCESSION 153

EXPRESS GRATITUDE 161

MOVEMENT OR EXERCISE 165

INSPIRED READING 167

TOPICAL BIBLE STUDY 169

DAILY DECLARATIONS AND AFFIRMATIONS (PART 1) 173

DAILY DECLARATIONS AND AFFIRMATIONS (PART 2) 177

VISUALIZATION 181

REFLECTION AND DO-OVERS 185

SPIRITUAL JOURNALING 187

FAITH IT FORWARD STORY 193

DISCOVERING SILENCE 197

INNER HEALING **203**

NEGATIVE SELF TALK 203

WHAT YOU CAN FEEL YOU CAN HEAL #2 209

PUTTING OFF PRAYER 213

WELCOMING PRAYER 217

PASSING THE BATON **225**

FOLLOW YOUR HEART- LET THE SPIRIT GUIDE YOUR ROUTINE 225

ON YOUR OWN WITH GOD 229

APPENDIX **235**

MORE DAILY DECLARATIONS 235

BLANK JOURNAL ENTRIES **240**

ABOUT THE AUTHOR 267

Preface

Are You Missing Out on the Greatest Relationships of Your Life!

If you've loved daily devotionals like *Jesus Calling* or lectures by Dr. Caroline Leaf who shares the science behind negative thoughts and how it relates to God and scripture, you'll love *The Christian Meditation Journal*. The journal will provide you with effective tools and spiritual disciplines to not only recognize your destructive thoughts, inner hurts, and pains, but more importantly, how to root them out so you can live daily with more love, peace, joy, and contentment.

Many Christians go to church, read their Bibles, and even pray, but did you know that most believers come up short when it comes to living their best lives! By that, I mean a life filled with more peace, joy, and freedom! Most are going through the motions of being a Christian, but many never experience the transformative nature of God that can change them through and through. Instead, they struggle to be good enough or try to work their way into pleasing God. However, the good news is a free gift to all, you need only receive it!

In Job 42: 5, Job declared after much suffering, *"I had only heard about you before, but now I have seen you with my own eyes." Like Job, are you ready to see God with "your own eyes?"*

No one is immune to tragedy or pain, but suffering is an option. We suffer when we carry our pain instead of releasing it and wholeheartedly putting our trust and faith in God.

If you are ready to stop playing church and become the church, your life must go through a transformation, and that transformation starts from within. It's not external, something that you seek outside of yourself. According to Luke 17:20," The kingdom of God is within you." If you want to have a flourishing and life-changing relationship with God, and yourself, the only place to go is within.

Now you might be thinking, how does that work? How do I go within? Is this some new age mumbo jumbo? Absolutely not. Even the scriptures say that "God is a Spirit and they that worship Him must worship Him in Spirit and truth. We go within by quieting our minds, stilling our bodies, opening our hearts, and dwelling in God's divine presence. In simplest terms, this is Christian meditation.

If you are not spending regular quiet time with God to release your burdens, restore your peace of mind, heal your pain and memories, squash your limiting beliefs or connect with God as well as yourself, you truly are missing out on the greatest relationships of your life, a deeper and thriving relationship with God and You!

Not only that, God desires fellowship with his children. God says in Jeremiah 29:13, *"You will seek me and find me when you search for me with all your heart."* I created The Christian Meditation Journal for this very purpose. To help believers seek God with their hearts and not just their minds.

The Christian Meditation Journal guides you step by step to creating a daily Christian meditation practice and a life-changing morning routine. The Bible says, "Draw close to God and He will draw closer to you." Right now, you are as close to God as you desire to be, but is that close enough for you? Are you ready for a new journey of self-discovery that only a daily meditation practice can bring? If so, the lessons, tools and spiritual disciplines you will learn in this journal will help you to:

- o   Renew your mind & overcome negative thinking
- o   Live with more peace, joy, and freedom
- o   Free yourself from toxic emotions
- o   Draw closer to God than you thought possible
- o   Heal inner wounds and let go of the past
- o   Develop a better relationship with yourself
- o   Grow deeper in your spiritual walk and journey

The Christian Meditation Journal is divided into five sections. These include:

Section # 1- Building a Foundation
In this section, you will learn the importance of spending personal time with God and dwelling in his presence through Biblical meditation. You'll also discover why spending time with God is so important in building your faith and keeping you strong in the Lord.

Section # 2- The Basics
In section 2, you will learn four spiritual practices that you must do every day to restore and maintain your overall health and well-being. This section also contains a series of guided Christian meditations audios that you can access to support you in building an effective practice.

Section # 3- Beyond the Basics

In section 3, Beyond the Basics, you'll learn 15 additional spiritual disciplines and how to use them to further enhance your life and help you grow on even deeper levels- mental, emotionally, and spiritually.

Section # 4- Inner Healing

In section 4, you'll be provided with tools to help you overcome negative self-talk, heal your pain, release the past, and let go of toxic thoughts and emotions that may be subconsciously crippling your life.

Section # 5- Passing the Baton

Now that you've completed the lessons of the first 4 sections, it's time for you to use the lessons and tools to create your own personal morning routine. This also includes additional blank journal entries for you to continue with your morning routine on your own.

After completing *The Christian Meditation Journal*, you'll feel renewed, cleansed, and closer to the Lord. This daily time with God will transform your life and your relationship with God forever.

Don't allow busyness and the things of this world to squeeze out the time you spend with God. Jesus told us to watch and pray, abide in Him, and to cast all of our cares upon him. If we want to thrive and not just survive, we need all the power of the Holy Spirit we can get. We must decrease so that God can increase in us and that comes from spending time with God and in his presence. The Christian Meditation Journal will guide you through this process easily and effortless, one day at a time. All you need to do is show up!

If you've been looking for a deeper and more fulfilling relationship with the Lord or even just to enhance your quiet time with Him, you'll want to give *The Christian Meditation Journal* a try.

You Are Only as Healthy as the Thoughts You Think!

"As a man thinks in his heart, so is he." – Proverbs 23:7

Many people approach health and wellness from many different perspectives. In general, we think that eating the right foods, living in a chemical-free environment, or even having a consistent exercise routine contribute greatly to how we feel, and to some extent this is true. However, according to the CDC and the World Health Organization, 80-85% of all disease has an emotional root! In reality, it is our dis-ease that is creating our bad health and most of our chronic illnesses.

Our thoughts are intricately connected to our emotions. We think and then we feel. This happens so instantaneously that we hardly recognize it. Have a bad thought and within moments, our emotions will follow suit.

You may feel a rush of anger, a dark cloud of depression hovering overhead, the tingling of anxiety, and many other bodily sensations.

Becoming aware of your thought life and then bringing every thought captive to the love, light, and principles of Christ, is the only way to true mental, emotional, and physical well-being. Food, exercise, and living a chemical-free life are important, but if your thoughts are dark or chronically negative or you are filled with anxiety or fear, you may be subconsciously sabotaging your very own health and well-being.

Matthew 6:22 declares, *"The eye is the lamp of the body. If your eyes are healthy, your whole body will be full of light."* Your eyes are the filters from which we see and experience the world. If your eyes are covered with all types of debris (emotional hurt, pain, anger, worry, limiting beliefs, and more), you'll obscure the very love and light that you desperately seek. True healing is more about removing the smudges from our minds and hearts that will then naturally allow the love and light of God to flow freely within us and around us.

Also, 2 Corinthians 7: 1 declares, "Therefore, since we have these promises, dear friends, let us purify ourselves from everything that contaminates body and spirit, perfecting holiness out of reverence for God." Notice that God puts the onus on us to purify our hearts and minds? Unfortunately, many Christians still live with the mental and emotional toxins of anger, fear, grieve, guilt and have never been internally cleansed. Our conscious, as well as sub-conscious mindsets, continue to rob us of the abundant life that Christ came to give us. Just like a daily shower to cleanse the body, we must consistently wash out the toxins that have taken residence in our minds.

Christian meditation brings awareness to what's going on inside of our heads, so we can begin to challenge the thoughts and beliefs that may be keeping us stuck. How do you know you are stuck? You feel it in your body. It's the difference between feeling happy and content or depressed and sad. These are the signals that God has given us to let us know if we have sound mental health.

The Christian Meditation Journal is a step by step guide into learning how to meditate as a Christian. You'll also be introduced to spiritual disciplines that promote spiritual growth and healing. You'll be guided easily and effortlessly through developing a meditation practice that can transform your life and relationship with God.

If you've ever wanted to learn how to meditate but didn't know where to start, wondered if meditation was for Christians, or wanted a structured program to get you started, this journal is for you.

As someone who has been teaching Christian meditation for over 10 years through my online courses, books, retreats, classes, and groups, I have seen and experienced first-hand the life-altering effects of dwelling in God's presence in the form of meditation. In fact, it was meditation integrated with scriptures that helped me overcome over 4-years of a deep depression when nothing else helped.

When you have the right tools, healing can take place. The best part is that you can learn and do it yourself! You don't have to remain a victim to your thoughts and emotions. By learning and following a few simple techniques that I will teach you in the journal, you can get your life back and have the tools necessary to heal yourself any time life happens.

Blessings, Rhonda Jones

Acknowledgments

To God, my source, strength, supply, and life's ultimate reward. Thank you for opening my eyes to what really matters most: love, peace, forgiveness, faith, and the present moment.

To my Mom, who is my biggest fan and who is one of the wisest women I know and who showed me that you can follow your dreams.

To my daughters for being the best friends a mom can have.

To my friends for asking the right questions and keeping me grounded.

To Tyler and Autumn, my grandchildren, for reminding me what it means to live in the present moment.

To my sister Janine because she is the kindest, most compassionate and loving human being I know, not in words but in deed.

To my Great Grandma, who is living it up with Jesus but still checking on me from time to time.

To my clients, customers, and subscribers who have encouraged and supported me in making this ministry something possible and special.

Introduction

How to use this journal? The Christian Meditation Journal is broken down into 5 components. These include building a foundation, the basics, beyond the basics, inner healing, and then lastly, passing the baton.

Each component builds upon the one before it. If possible, work through each lesson per day. Some of the lessons are longer than others, especially in the beginning. If you don't have time to complete a lesson in one setting, find a good place to stop and then return to it the next day.

The journal is designed to help you establish an ongoing daily Christian meditation practice by introducing you to different activities and spiritual disciplines that will empower and change your life. After completing the foundational section and the basics, feel free to move around to topics that you feel you need to explore, even out of order. It's all about listening to your spirit. Then go back to where you left off.

This journal is a complete revision of my previous book, "A Date with God" with a new format and lots of new content to help you design a meditation and journaling practice that can last for years to come. By the time you reach the end of this journal, you will have a daily practice and a plethora of tools to cultivate a life of more peace, joy, and purpose. – Rhonda Jones

building a spiritual foundation

Building a Spiritual Foundation

Who's Doing the Work?

Has your walk with God become stagnant? Do you desire to do God's will but you're not really sure what it is? Are you desiring a closer, more intimate walk with God but can't figure out the steps to get you there? Or maybe you desperately desire to be used of God, to see his miracles work in your life, but instead, you often feel powerless and weak in your faith.

The God we read about in the Bible is the God of miracles, power, healing, and revelation. Everywhere that Jesus trekked there was a demonstration of his power. Yet, why aren't we seeing more of God's supernatural demonstrations in our own lives as well as the churches we attend? What are we missing? What do we need in order to really do the works of Jesus?

Mark 6: 17-18 states, *"And these signs will accompany those who believe: In my name they will drive out demons; they will speak in new tongues; they will pick up snakes with their hands; and when they drink deadly poison, it will not hurt them at all; they will place their hands on sick people, and they will get well."*

Could it be that the reason we are missing a real manifestation of God is our failure to be "one" with God in mind, body, and spirit?" Jesus said in John 10:30 that "I and the Father are one." Then in John 14:10, Jesus declares, *"Don't you believe that I am in the Father and that the Father is in me? The words I say to you I do not speak on my own authority. Rather, it is the Father, living in me, who is doing his work."*

Maybe we need to ask ourselves, "Who's doing the work in us?" Is it God through the power of the Holy Spirit or have we pretty much set out to do it all on our own? Experiencing God's power in our lives isn't about mustering up a lot of emotion or even increasing our faith. Unleashing God's anointing with signs following is in direct proportion to how much space God takes up within us, literally. If there is less of us, then there is more of God, and if more of us, then less of God. Too often we put God in these scheduled compartments like an activity on our to-do list. We may attend church regularly or participate in many ministry activities, yet in all honesty, what type of relationship are we really building with God? Jesus in Matthew 15: 18, *"These people come near to me with their mouth and honor me with their lips, but their hearts are far from me. Their worship of me is based on merely human rules they have been taught."*

I think we often forget that God is a spiritual being operating beyond the realm of our human understanding. Because spiritualism has been associated with the occult and demonic practices, we're afraid to truly embrace the spiritual nature of God. However, the Bible is filled with supernatural occurrences of God that we can't dismiss, but that are rarely seen today.

Since the fault cannot lie with God, then it must lie with us. Jesus said, the harvest is ready, but the labors are few. Instead of being about God's business, we are rapidly pursuing our own. We are often immune or deaf to the spirit of God wanting to manifest himself through us and are guilty of quenching the spirit to our own demise.

"But an hour is coming, and now is, when the true worshipers will worship the Father in spirit and truth; for such people the Father seeks to be His worshipers." (John 4:24) I believe it's time for God's people to wake up and get busy, not for building their own kingdom, but the kingdom of God! And the first place we must start is in His Presence, surrendered and bearing all before Him and making ourselves available for his use.

If we truly want to be that light that draws the unsaved to Christ, people need to see God in us. When Moses came down from the Mt. of Olives, his body glistened so much with the presence of God that the people couldn't even look at him.

Just like Moses, the way we open ourselves to the indwelling presence of God's Spirit and His likeness is to spend intimate time with Him. Sunday worship service and bible study just aren't enough. God wants to fellowship with us. Jesus tells us in Revelations 3:20, *"Behold, I stand at the door and knock; if anyone hears My voice and opens the door, I will come into Him and will dine with Him, and he with Me."*

Has God been knocking at the door of your heart, but you've been too busy or too self-absorbed to listen or let Him in? Doesn't your heart desire to dine with the Master, sit at His feet, and learn from Him, but you think you just can't spare the time?

Journaling- Write it Out:

1. Who is doing most of the work in your life? You or God?

_____

_____

_____

_____

2. Has it been difficult relinquishing control? If so, why?

_____

_____

_____

_____

3. Why do you want to spend more time with God?

_____

_____

_____

_____

4. How do you think establishing a daily meditation time with God will change your life?

_____

_____

_____

_____

5. What has been standing in the way of you scheduling this time into your day?

_____

_____

_____

_____

Closing Prayer:

Heavenly Father help me to relinquish control of my life to you. This walk-through life should not be burdensome or a constant struggle, but filled with your love, peace, and joy, as I live in alignment with you. Father teach me how to decrease so that your Spirit can have greater influence and authority in my life. I desire that you do the work, and I simply join in and follow. Amen.

Are You Ready to Make an Appointment?

I believe we are living in the last of the last days. Satan's plan is accelerating yet the church appears to be sleeping. It's time to wake up as our redemption draws near. We must draw closer to God if we are to stand in the days of temptation. While we are busy pursuing our own endeavors, the enemy continues to strengthen his strongholds and take away our freedoms.

As wages are being reduced, workloads have increased. As with the Israelites, satan will do anything he can to keep us from abiding in the presence of God. He knows that if we spend time in God's presence we will be changed into the very image of Christ. With Christ's image comes power from on high. Not our power, but the very power of God living and operating through us. Therefore, he'll find any and every distraction possible to keep you from seeking God and spending time, one-on-one, with Him.

Spending time with God through intimate praise, worship, meditation, and prayer changes us from the inside out. It's not us, but God doing the work. In order to experience God's joy, peace, purpose, and fulfillment we must continually renew our minds from the contaminants and delusions of the world. This is accomplished by meditating on Christ and His empowering teachings and eliminating (through the renewal of the Holy Spirit) toxic attitudes, thoughts, fears, and mindsets that keep us bound.

By committing, making an appointment, to spend time with God as often as possible, we learn about the transformative power of Christ's Spirit and discover that the love, joy, provision, and fulfillment we seek comes from Him and not outer pursuits.

With a consistent Date with God, an appointment to dwell in His presence, worship His character, and meditate on His word, as well as connect with our own inner spirit, we can accomplish more and struggle less. We can learn what it really means to give up striving in our own strength and put our trust and faith in God alone.

If you want to usher in God's presence and power in your life, you must seek a habitation of God in your life, in fact, in your very being. By habitation, we allow God to live in and through us as a vessel surrendered to do His will.

It's no more I, but Christ living in me and through me. Paul declared, *"I have been crucified with Christ and I no longer live, but Christ lives in me. The life I now live in the body, I live by faith in the Son of God, who loved me and gave himself for me."* Are you ready to make that appointment?

Journaling- Write it Out:

1. Has your life or distractions hindered your time with God? Can you identify them?

   _____

   _____

   _____

   _____

2. Do you feel the spirit of God pulling on you to come into His secret place?

   _____

   _____

   _____

   _____

3. What toxic thoughts, emotions, attitudes, or mindsets may need to be cleansed from your mind and heart?

   _____

   _____

   _____

4. What does it mean for you to be crucified with Christ?

_____

_____

_____

_____

Closing Prayer:

Heavenly Father, as the psalmist wrote, "My heart and soul seek after the living God;" however, I have often allowed distractions, busyness, and the cares of this world get in the way of intimate time with you. Father, today I make a new commitment to make spending time with you a priority. Amen

Seeking Creation vs. the Creator?

Are your pursuits leading you away from God instead of to Him? Are you on a continual search for peace, joy, prosperity, and fulfillment by pursuing the things of this world? Does your security come from your possessions, and if you lost them all tomorrow, would your faith in God sustain you? These are tough questions, questions I had to answer myself.

I found myself looking for strategies to possess the things I wanted. There is no scarcity of programs for every problem, and it's so easy to fall prey to them. Many seem just what we've been looking for, but in the end, we feel just as empty and confused as when we began.

Recently, in meditative prayer and stillness, God asked me a simple question. Why are you working so hard to find the answers, when all I have asked you to do is SEEK ME FIRST and everything you need will be added unto you? By 'everything,' God will meet my needs and fulfill the truest desires of my heart, for He said He knows what we need before we even ask. Not what WE think we need, but what He knows we need to satisfy the longings and emptiness in our hearts. Jesus told us in Matthew 6 to continually pursue His Lordship when so often we pursue the things of this world.

I believe that by spending intimate time with God, we can accomplish more than a lifetime of striving in our own strength. Join me and others in the pursuit of Jesus and watch your life change forever.

But Seek Ye First the Kingdom of God…
How many times have you read Matthew 6:33-34?

> *"But seek first his kingdom and his righteousness, and all these things will be given to you as well. Therefore, do not worry about tomorrow, for tomorrow will worry about itself."*

If you are like most believers, you probably have this verse memorized. Now here comes the big question, "Are you doing it?" Or are you attempting to meet your needs, in your own way, according to your own understanding?

This is that classic scripture that we all know, but we rarely do, at least the majority of the time. Instead, we are busy trying to make things happen in our own strength. Whether it's to find a job, maintain a business, deal with spouses or children, or get our needs met, we rarely go to God first.

Usually, it is after much struggle and defeat that we raise our hands and surrender it all to the Lord. I think that is when Jesus says, "Okay, about time, now you're ready to give it to me. I'll get to work."

But why can't we just do that in the beginning? Think of all of the worries, stress, time, and energy we can save. Think of all the joy, peace, and laughter we wouldn't have to forfeit. I believe the reason we just don't seek God first is that we have been conditioned not to. Over and over we are programmed to believe that it is hard work that pays off and that being idle is laziness. Many people feel guilty when they aren't doing something. They don't even really know how to relax and "just be," especially in our American culture. No, instead we are told if you want to prosper and get ahead, you must "work, work, and work some more." God says in Haggai, 1:6, *"You have planted much, but harvested little. You eat but never have enough. You drink but never have your fill. You put on clothes but are not warm. You earn wages, only to put them in a purse with holes in it."* Could this be the curse for pursuing material goods instead of pursuing God first?

It's no wonder when God tells us in Matthew 6 to *"Seek first the kingdom of God and His righteousness and ALL these things will be added unto you,"* we have a hard time believing it. However, there is also a second question to be considered when it comes to allowing God to provide for us. Are we more interested in seeking the creation or the Creator? Sometimes seeking God isn't so much about standing in faith as it is obtaining the material goods that we've also been conditioned to pursue for our happiness.

Romans 14:17 declares, *"For the kingdom of God is not a matter of eating and drinking [material goods], but of righteousness, peace and joy in the Holy Spirit."*

According to the previous verse, not even the rudimentary pleasures of eating and drinking bring true happiness, but instead it is being filled with God's Spirit and bathing in His righteousness, peace, and joy.

So how do we get there? Where can we find this perpetual peace and joy that eludes so many of us, even Christians?

What does it mean to seek God first and how do we go about it? That is what The Christian Meditation Journal attempts to answer, but it goes even further because not only does it tell you, it shows you.

If we want to be successful in our walk with God, we need a paradigm shift. It may require a whole new way of thinking. Jesus made it clear in Luke 16:13, *"You can't serve both God and money."*

That doesn't mean that God wants us poor and wretched because many of the disciples of Jesus were wealthy people; however, their sufficiency came from God and not themselves. Their success was a by-product of serving and seeking God and not the other way around.

In Mark Chapter 10, the rich younger ruler, turned away from God feeling sad because he wouldn't let go of his possessions to follow the Lord, not understanding that seeking God, and abiding in His presence, was exactly what he yearned for.

It was the very thing he needed to find "peace and joy in the Holy Spirit." Yet, instead, he leaned to his own understanding, as many of us do, and continued down the illusion of the American Dream that includes toil, deception, emptiness, and despair. Mark 8:36 reminds us, *"For what does it profit a man to gain the whole world and forfeit his soul?"*

Being self-employed for a large portion of my life has given me a perspective on trusting God to meet my needs that I believe the average person just hasn't experienced. When you don't have a steady paycheck that you can count on, it is so easy to get into fear. If you don't train your mind to trust the Lord and to cast down every vain imagination, you really could go crazy. Yet, after doing a lot of self-reflection, one thing I realized was that even though I asserted that was trusting God, I really wasn't. Even though on the surface, it might have looked like I had peace, underneath it all, I was just waiting for the bottom to be pulled from under me, and finally, it happened!

Although in the beginning I was upset with God for allowing this, I knew that this was necessary for me to "really" seek and see God as my source and supplier instead of the internet, marketing efforts, website traffic, the perfect website, my Google rankings, promotions, and all the strategies I put into place.

I can honestly tell you that the more I tried to fix things, the worst they got. I was living Haggai 1:6 over and over. I had to come face to face with my fear. Would I really make it? Would God really pull me through? Was He there? Did He really care, were some questions I grappled with? This would be a test for me!

I had to do the paradigm shift that I spoke about earlier. My standard of living was somewhat reduced. I couldn't buy everything I wanted when I wanted. I had to change my residence to fit my budget. For a while, I felt like a failure, but God was doing something in me.

He was changing my perspective. He was letting me know that my self-worth had nothing to do with what I possessed, but instead, it came from Him. It didn't matter if I had $5.00 or $15,000 in the bank, I was important, loved, and worthy, and I could hold my head just as high.

For me, this was pure freedom, but it was even more because I truly experienced God as my Jehovah Jireh, my provider. Luke 12:15 states it perfectly, "Watch out! Be on your guard against all kinds of greed; life does not consist in an abundance of possessions." I think we as Christians need to hear this. This generation has grown up listening to the prosperity gospel that often equates wealth with godliness. Unfortunately, striving for material goods has its clinches buried deep in the church as well.

With everything against me, God was still for me, and He proved it again and again. For me Matthew 6 rang true, *"Seek ye first the kingdom of God and all things will be added unto you. Therefore, do not worry about tomorrow, for tomorrow will worry about itself."*

The second part of the verse is just as important as the first, "do not worry about tomorrow." God provided, but He didn't give me a windfall. He didn't give me a big savings account, stocks and bonds, or a cushy new job with a high salary.

Instead, God provided one day at a time, meeting this need and then the next. I know that some of you are thinking, "Well I need a lot more security than that!" That is the trap, the deceptive lie that keeps us from seeking and trusting God and instead trying to venture out on our own. I was in bondage, but now I am free. There are things I want to be restored and I'm praying for, but my goal is not the stuff, but maintaining that peace and joy that only the Holy Spirit can give, which comes with an authentic and intimate relationship with Christ through seeking and fellowshipping with Him.

I am praying that *The Christian Meditation Journal* will start you on the journey of breaking free from the pursuits of this world and seeking what is really going to make your soul sing and flourish. If your walk with God feels "dead" or in a coma, maybe it is time to seek God with all your heart, soul, and strength.

When we give to God, He gives back to us, sometimes a one-hundred-fold. Luke 6:36 says, Give, and it will be given to you. A good measure, pressed down, shaken together and running over, will be poured into your lap. For with the measure you use, it will be measured to you." I believe this verse applies equally to giving our time to the Lord and the first fruits of our day.

Jesus said in Mark 10:28-32 – *"Then Peter began to say unto him, Lo, we have left all, and have followed thee. And Jesus answered and said, Verily I say unto you, there is no man that hath left house, or brethren, or sisters, or father, or mother, or wife, or children, or lands, for my sake, and the gospel's, but he shall receive a hundredfold now in this time, houses, and brethren, and sisters, and mothers, and children, and lands, with persecutions; and in the world to come eternal life. But many that are first shall be last; and the last first."*

32

Can you give it all up to follow Jesus? Specifically, can you give up some of your time to fellowship with Him consistently? By trying to make ourselves first, Jesus said, we become last. When we follow Jesus with our whole heart, blessings are in store for us, but not because we pursued them, because God blesses those who have a heart for Him, not just in word but in deed.

A date with God is just the beginning of creating a daily appointment with God that has the potential to change your life and your relationship with the Lord forever. When you spend time with God in praise, prayer, meditation, and devotion, there is no telling what God will do in your life. Each day can become an adventure. Watching God answer the prayers you list in your journal will create a desire to pray even more.

Taking all your cares and burdens to God, instead of carrying them around with you, will become automatic. Your time with God can become your comfort in the storm and your fortress in time of need. You'll find yourself craving this time and wondering how you ever lived without it. As you draw closer to God, He will draw closer to you.

There isn't a better place to be. As you continue to read, you'll discover even more of the benefits of a regular date with God. Tomorrow, it's time for you to get "centered" in the Son.

Journaling- Write it Out:

1. In what ways have you sought the creation instead of the creator?

_____

_____

_____

_____

2. In what areas of life should you be seeking God first?

_____

_____

_____

_____

3. What do you think would be God's idea of a successful life?

_____

_____

_____

_____

4. What paradigm shift do you need to make so that you and God are on the same page?

_____

_____

_____

_____

Closing Prayer:

Heavenly Father, it's so easy to get caught up in this world and begin to pursue the creation instead of the creator. Although these things may seem tempting to the eye and nourishing to the soul, they can never satisfy the spiritual longings in our hearts. Lord, help me to break any attachments I have to this material world that is passing away. Amen. I desire to seek the treasure that is in heaven that flows from an intimate relationship with you. "The only thing that matters is faith expressing itself through love."

Getting Centered in the Son

There is only one you! You are unique and valuable and have something special to offer the world. Don't get caught up on that word "world" though. Your world right now might be your family, your spouse, a small group of believers, or a ministry in your church. Regardless of the size of your world, it centers around you, just like the planets center around the sun. Without the light and energy of the sun, the earth could not survive or sustain life. Once the sun goes out, its lights out for the planets as well. You are the sun of your world, and your planets are only as mentally, spiritually, and emotionally healthy as you are. You can't give what you don't have. You can't sustain life if all the life is drained out of you. God is our sun. Not only is He our creator, but He is our life force. We derive everything we need to survive from Him alone. We may think we get what we need from other channels, but if we go back to the source, it's God, because without Him nothing can exist.

Our health and well-being are also a by-product of God. The more we are in tune with God's peace, joy, and love, the greater our capacity will be to manifest these characteristics in our own life. If we aren't experiencing God's love, how can we share with others?

I am sure that you would agree that many believers, maybe even you, are depleted in the love, joy, and peace department. At certain times in our lives, we can sense the dark clouds that are blocking God's light from shining through.

I think it is so interesting that places like Seattle and Washington have the highest percentages of depression. Out of the 12 calendar months, 9 of these months include rain and dark clouds that block the rays of the sun. We can see just how important the sun is to our emotional well-being. We can use the same analogy to understand how important the Son, God's Son, is to our spiritual health and well-being.

Even though we can predict the orbit of the sun, we can't always predict the circumstances that will block its light: the rain, fog, storms, hurricanes, blizzards, etc. We know that Fall and Winter will bring the harshest weather of the season, so we can prepare; however, with so many variables, we never really know what we're going to get until it's usually right upon us.

That's why it's always good to be prepared and keep plenty of firewood, blankets, candles, flashlights, matches, and whatever else we need to make it through.

It is the same with God and His Son. We never know when the dark clouds of depression, anxiety, restlessness, anger, jealousy, insecurity, fear, sadness, grief, worry, and the like are going to strike. Just like with the weather, we want to be prepared.

Jude 1:20 tells us to build ourselves up in our most holy faith. When the storms hit, it's not the time to run out and buy supplies. In the parable of the 10 virgins who were waiting for the bridegroom to return, five of them were ill-prepared, and when the bridegroom arrived, they didn't have enough oil in their lamps to greet him.

Similar to our own spiritual health and well-being, isn't it better to maintain peace of mind than try to overcome worry, fear, and doubt? Wouldn't you rather avoid depression than try to conquer it? Wouldn't it be better to keep your joy rather than have to find it again? By staying connected with the Son and getting rid of the dark clouds that surface, when they surface, we can maintain a healthy mind and spirit today and every day.

It would be amiss to say that dark clouds aren't going to come; they are just a part of the seasons of life. However, the key is what you do with the clouds when they come. You can just stand underneath them and get rained on, ruining your hair and your day, or you can choose to find shelter and solace and move out of their way. That shelter and solace are in the Son. Through God's principles, promises, and spiritual disciplines, we can subdue the clouds and push them out of our mental skies and consciousness. It's like having your own spiritual umbrella. You can choose to be a victim or a victor, to be an overcomer or to be overcome.

Journaling- Write it Out:

1. Who in your world of influence depends upon you to be a beacon of light?

_____

_____

_____

2. What types of dark clouds are raining on your spiritual parade?

_____

_____

_____

_____

3. What are you doing currently to get out of the spiritual rain or from under dark clouds?

_____

_____

_____

_____

4. How are you feeling encouraged to draw closer to the Son for your strength and well-being?

_____

_____

_____

Closing Prayer:

Father God, Jesus, and the Holy Spirit, you are my beautiful and radiant sun. Without you, I am hollow and empty and often overshadowed with the dark clouds of depression, guilt, unworthiness, and pain. Father, today I invite your glorious light of peace, love, healing, and joy into my life. As your light dissolves and dissipates all darkness within me, I pray that I shall become a beacon of love and light to those surrounding me. I let my light shine brightly in you. Amen.

Manna for Today

There is a common thread throughout the Bible that shows us that God operates in day-tight compartments. For example, God gave the children of Israel only enough manna for a day. Any leftover manna turned to maggots. Also, Jesus told us not to worry about tomorrow, but to keep our attention only on the present moment, today! It is said that yesterday is history and the future is a mystery. Therefore, what you did yesterday may or may not carry you through today. Paul said, "I die daily" (I Corinthians 15:31), meaning each day is a new beginning to re-invent ourselves and our lives.

Each day, we must connect with our source and drive away the clouds that come floating by. If you expect last week's supplies to sustain you, you're going to come up lacking. Just as we deplete our physical supplies, we also deplete our spiritual and emotional storerooms. Your time with Jesus last week may not be enough to carry you through weeks ahead. Just like you need your daily supplements, you need your daily time with God if you are going to keep your spiritual strength to conquer every storm that comes your way.

If you were giving your children their vitamins one morning, and they said, "No thanks, Mom. I took it yesterday," you might laugh and tell them, "Sweetie, that vitamin was for yesterday; this one is for today." The same logic is true regarding our meals, exercise, hygiene, and work.

Although they can have an accumulating effect, once you stop, you slowly, or sometimes quickly, regress in the opposite direction. Your spiritual well-being is no different. What you put in is what you get out! Creating a daily date with God is your lifeline to the Son that will help you stay mentally, emotionally, and spiritually strong in spite of your circumstances. Now and then, despite your best efforts to prepare, there may be a storm of such magnitude that it will knock you off your feet, but it won't keep you down, at least not for long. Just like David who slew Goliath, one good victory helps to propel and prepare us for the next one. Your time with God is your arsenal against the works of the enemy as well as the trials of life. It will help you to live above your circumstances, above the clouds, and just bask in the light of the Son and His promises: love, joy, peace, patience, trust, and contentment.

If you're going to spend time with God, why not make it as effective as possible? Use your time with God to empower you for greatness. You are more than a conqueror in Christ Jesus who loves you. You just need to put on God's armor and take out your weapons. God said if you use them, you will have the victory.

The operative word here is "use" them. You must use the weapons or tools daily, if they are to work for you. Start putting them into use today and watch as your life and relationship with God changes forever.

Isn't that worth an hour or two occasionally, of your day? You might think you don't have this much time to devote to God every day. Didn't Jesus say in Matthew 6:33, *"Seek ye first the kingdom of God and his righteousness and everything you need shall be added unto you"*? If you aren't seeking God to meet your needs according to His plan, you're going about it all wrong.

You may be seeking the creation instead of the Creator. Jesus said to seek Him first, and He will add unto us what we need. As I stated in the preface, last year during my own time with God, His Spirit said to me loud and clear, "Rhonda, why are you making this so difficult! Seek Me instead of seeking solutions."

Too many of God's children are seeking solutions instead of seeking God, and it's leaving them tired and disillusioned. There have been times in my life that God just threw me an unexpected blessing. I wasn't even looking for it, but He knew the desires of my heart. I didn't have to strive for it or work hard to make it happen. God just added it unto me, and I just had to receive it as a gift and walk in faith.

Spending quality time with God may cut your "doing" in half. Not only can God bless you with the desires of your heart, but He'll keep your heart free from the toxic emotions of worry, fear, and negativity. Just that alone is a good, even great, reason to give God a portion of your time every day.

Finally, I'd like to discuss legalism for a moment, because it always wants to raise its ugly head and turn everything into a "must" or "shall do!" We have liberty in Jesus Christ. God doesn't require us to do anything to receive our salvation but believe. That's the basics, but there is so much more, so who wants to stay there? My desire is not that you spend time with God regularly because you have to. I want you to do it because:

It makes you feel great.

You have more peace and joy as a result.

Your relationship with Christ is growing.

You love sensing God's presence.

It helps you in your relationships.

It helps you have more good days than bad days.

You want more intimacy with God.

You can do less and accomplish more.

God wants to fellowship with you.

It might change your perspective.

It will help you slow down.

It will help you break your addiction to the delusions and lies of the world.

It's time with just you and God.

You need to nurture you.

You are worth it!

I don't spend time with God because I "want" to; I spend time with God because I "need" to. It is my daily medicine for good spiritual health and well-being. I also do it because I love dwelling in God's presence and feeling His love surround me. It is my "me" time, time to love and nurture me because I'm worth it. It also helps me to be the best I can be for me and those in my world because when I'm spiritually and mentally grounded, I pass that on to them.

Journaling: Write It Out:

1. Why might spending time with God irregularly be unproductive?

_____

_____

_____

_____

2. Why does God want us to live in day-tight compartments?

_____

_____

_____

_____

3. What are "your" best reasons for spending time with God regularly?

_____

_____

_____

_____

Closing Prayer:

Father God, you don't desire a sometime relationship with me. The longer I am away from you, the more depleted I feel. Father help me to see this time with you as precious and necessary. You are the well that springs forth from my heart that replenishes me daily. I purpose to dedicate each and every day to you. Amen.

But Why One Hour? Let's Look at Scripture!

Mark 14: 32 reads, *"They [Jesus and the disciples] went to a place called Gethsemane, and Jesus said to His disciples, 'Sit here while I pray… Stay here and keep watch.'"* Then, verse 37 reads, He [Jesus] returned to His disciples and found them sleeping. *"Simon,"* He said to Peter, *"Are you sleeping? Couldn't you keep watch for one hour?"*

"Watch and pray so that you will not fall into temptation. The spirit is willing, but the flesh is weak." (Mark 14:38). Once more, He went away and prayed the same thing. When He came back, He, again, found them sleeping. They did not know what to say to Him. Returning the third time, He said to them, *"Are you still sleeping and resting? Enough! The hour has come."* (Mark 14:41).

I think it is also interesting that Jesus went and prayed to the Father at least 3 times in one night concerning the major event that was to take place. It is okay and sometimes necessary to intercede again and again regarding a situation. On past occasions, I remember praying until I had a release or until my faith was so strong, I could let it go and put my trust fully in God. That doesn't always happen with quick and superficial prayers. I sometimes believe we need to reach deep into our own heart before we can touch the heart of God.

Jeremiah 29:13 says, *"You will seek me and find me when you search for me with all your heart."* But what does that mean? How do we seek and pursue God, with all our heart, all our soul, and all our strength? Many faithful servants of God would have us believe that to grow in greater intimacy with Christ we should 1) attend more church services, 2) get busy for God by signing up for more outreaches and committees, and 3) pray longer and harder. These all seem like wonderful and godly tasks, but I believe there are five key elements to pursuing God.

These include, abiding in God's presence by spending time with Him, renewing our minds and purifying our hearts, preparing our hearts for His return, putting on God's full armor, and meditating on God's Word and hiding it in our hearts. I'll discuss each of those as we move forward.

Journaling- Write it Out:

1. Why is it important to spend time with God regularly, preferably daily?

_____

_____

_____

_____

2. What do you think would be the accumulating effects of you spending regular time with God?

_____

_____

_____

_____

3. What was the significance in Jesus asking the disciples to pray for one hour?

_____

_____

_____

_____

4. Write down a situation recently that would take more than a superficial prayer here and there to resolve?

_____

_____

_____

_____

Closing Prayer:

Father God, so often I have a desire to spend time with you, but I give into temptation or the desires of my human nature. I know that there is no better place than in your divine presence. Today, I make a fresh commitment to spend time with you. Even if I can't devote a full hour, I know that whatever time I give to you will have a profound impact on my life. Thank you, Jesus for your patience with me and helping me to actively purpose and wait upon you. Amen.

Pursuing God # 1

#1- Abide in God's Presence and Spend time with Him

We read, in Genesis, that at the cool of every day, Adam walked in the garden with God (implied in 3:8). In John 15:5, Jesus said, *"I am the vine and you are the branches. If you remain in me, and I in you, you will bear much fruit; apart from me you can do nothing."*

There are no short cuts to building intimacy in relationships. If you rarely spend time with those you say you love, you're not sending the message that they are important to you. Although God is a Spirit, we can still connect with Him. That connection comes by abiding in His presence. God's presence is all around us. Sometimes we can feel it, and other times we can observe the beauty of God in nature. Abiding in Christ requires being still and seeking God from the heart instead of the head.

Another aspect of abiding in God's presence and spending time with Him includes entering into God's rest. Hebrews 4: 1-3 declares, *"Therefore since the promise of entering His rest still stands, let us be careful that none of you be found to have fallen short of it. For we also have had the good news proclaimed to us, just as they did; but the message they heard was of no value to them, because it was not mixed with faith. Now we who have believed enter that rest..."*

God has a rest for His children, but we must enter into this rest by faith. Why by faith? Many believers are afraid to release the reins or control over their lives. They don't really trust God to meet their needs, and instead of entering into God's rest, they persist to succeed in their own effort. Yet, even God on the 7th day of creation rested from all His work. *"For somewhere, He has spoken about the seventh day in these words: "on the seventh day God rested from all His works."* (Hebrews 4:4)

"There remains, then, a sabbath-rest for the people of God; for anyone who enters God's rest also rests from their works, just as God did from His. Let us, therefore, make every effort to enter that rest, so that no one will perish by following their example of disobedience."(Hebrews 4:9-11)

The act of entering into God's rest may take on different meanings to different people. For some, entering into God's rest may suggest the need to stop striving and laboring in their own effort and to completely rely upon (and trust) the Lord with everything. For others, entering into God's rest may signify a Sabbath day or a frequent time of "just being" with God and abiding in His Presence.

It may mean to cease from everyday duties and labor to reflect upon the Lord, His presence, and His Word. From a physical standpoint, our bodies, as well as our minds, need scheduled times of rest to recharge and regain our strength and resolve.

A date with God provides us with the opportunity to recharge our spiritual and physical batteries to prepare us for the days ahead.

2- Renewing Our Minds and Purifying Our Hearts

Did you know that God puts the responsibility on us to purify our minds and cleanse our hearts of everything that will distract us, weigh us down, attack our faith, and hinder our relationship with Him? This doesn't happen without effort on our part.

Just read the verses below:

2 Corinthians 10:5 tells us to cast down arguments and every high thing that exalts itself against the knowledge of God, bringing every thought into captivity to the obedience of Christ.

2 Corinthians 7:1 declares, "Therefore, since we have these promises, dear friends, let us purify ourselves from everything that contaminates body and spirit, perfecting holiness out of reverence for God."

Hebrews 12:1 says, "Therefore since we are surrounded by such a great cloud of witnesses, let us throw off everything that hinders and the sin and that so easily entangles, and let us run with perseverance the race marked out before us."

Colossians 3:5 tells believers to "put to death, therefore, whatever belongs to your earthly nature …you must also rid yourself of all such things as these: anger, rage, malice, slander, and filthy language from your lips."

We can ask God to cleanse and purify our hearts, but generally, this will come in the form of trials and tests. We don't know what is in our hearts until we face difficult circumstances.

We may think we have faith, that is until we lose our job or some other form of security. We may think we're kind and loving until we're faced with an unrelenting enemy or wronged in some way. It is these types of circumstances or events that uncover our true character or the condition of our hearts.

Therefore, when we notice or discover we are being selfish, unloving, fearful, or angry, God tells us to cast down, throw off, purify, and rid ourselves of such behaviors. Spending time with God continually, will help us to become more aware of our true nature.

In quietness and stillness, we learn to become the observer of our thoughts, reactions, and emotions. This is very powerful because instead of reacting to every circumstance by default, we learn to make conscious choices. In reality, what we're learning is to take power over our thoughts and behaviors by bringing them under the authority of Christ.

Checking in and Meditation (Dwelling in God's Presence), which we'll cover later, provides a wonderful opportunity to observe our inner voice and emotions and release or take authority over them. Sometimes that might mean turning these over to God and asking Him to heal you. Once we have become familiar or aware of our inner dialogue, we can offer these to God in prayer, and by faith, receive our healing and restoration.

#3- Meditate on God's Word and Hide it in our Heart

Jesus said, "You shall know the truth and the truth shall make you free." (John 8:32).

Joshua 1:8 declares, "Keep this book of the law always on your lips; meditate on it day and night, so that you may be careful to do everything written in it. Then you will be prosperous and successful."

We must consistently and, if possible, daily, feed upon God's Word to help us cancel the delusions of this world. If you are a believer who's looking for more than a traditional church experience, it is going to require going deeper with God. Many of us want a great relationship with God, but we're not willing to put in the time and effort to make it happen.

Jesus is always knocking at the door of our hearts, but we either don't hear it, don't recognize it, or we ignore it altogether. It takes a strong believer to weed through the distractions of daily living and sit at the Master's feet. We'd much rather be a productive Martha than an abiding Mary.

Our society frowns on idleness. We always just have to be doing something, even if that something isn't going to amount to a hill of beans. Many believers will be surprised to find out that all their frantic activity wasn't even a part of God's purpose for their lives.

Unfortunately, they didn't stop long enough or take the time to find out. God has a hope and a plan for each of His children (Jeremiah 29:11), but if we never make an appointment with the Boss, how will we know what it is?

Instead, we go after this and that and usually miss out on vital information, the very information we needed to get the job done or go to the next level.

You might be saying to yourself, "Well, I pray every day and read my Bible." Do you know that you're still 'doing' something? When do you just be still and let God love on you? When are you quiet enough to listen and hear the still small voice of the Spirit? Spending time with God is a two-way street. We miss out when we don't allow God to fill us and transforms us with His Spirit.

My desire in writing this book and journal is to encourage believers to commit to spending quiet time with God, abiding in His presence, preparing for His return (next day's topic), purifying their heart, and meditating on His Word.

Journaling- Write it Out:

1. What is something in this section that resonated with you most?

_____

_____

_____

_____

2. What are some ways you can enter into God's rest on a regular basis?

_____

_____

_____

_____

3. List an area or two that YOU need to purify your heart or mind?

_____

_____

_____

4. Do you struggle with just being still? Where do you think this comes from?

_____

_____

_____

_____

Closing Prayer:

Father God, so many times I put the responsibility upon you to change me or my circumstances. Or, I frantically try to do these things in my own strength. Although you put the onus on me to purify my heart and mind, I can't do it alone. Help me to see the areas in my heart and life that need a shift, even an overhaul. I invite you into these areas. Fill me more and more with your love and light. Remove any darkness hidden within me. Amen.

Pursuing God # 2
#4- Preparing for Jesus's Return

I believe that a great majority of the western church is asleep. There is so much happening around us, and I'm hard pressed to find many ministers talking about it today. Recently, I've been reading Revelations regarding the seven churches.

Revelation 3: 14-22 declares: To the angel of the church in Laodicea write:

"These are the words of the Amen, the faithful and true witness, the ruler of God's creation. I know your deeds, that you are neither cold nor hot. I wish you were either one or the other! So, because you are lukewarm—neither hot nor cold—I am about to spit you out of my mouth. You say, 'I am rich; I have acquired wealth and do not need a thing.' But you do not realize that you are wretched, pitiful, poor, blind and naked. I counsel you to buy from me gold refined in the fire so you can become rich, and white clothes to wear, so you can cover your shameful nakedness; and salve to put on your eyes so you can see.

Those whom I love I rebuke and discipline. So be earnest and repent. Here I am! I stand at the door and knock. If anyone hears my voice and opens the door, I will come in and eat with that person, and they with me.

To the one who is victorious, I will give the right to sit with me on my throne, just as I was victorious and sat down with my Father on his throne. Whoever has ears, let them hear what the Spirit says to the churches."

To this church, Jesus says, *"You think you are rich and wealthy, but you are wretched, pitiful, blind and poor."* Why would Jesus say this? I believe because many believers are more concerned about their worldly affairs than they are with the kingdom of God. We have become accustomed to trying to serve both God and mammoth (money). We have sold out to the American Dream. Also, instead of being in the world but not of the world, we have allowed the deceptive tenets of evil to creep in, entangle, and put us in bondage.

Jesus tells the church at Ephesus, *"You have forsaken the love you had at first. Consider how far you have fallen! Repent and do the things you did at first."*

I am also guilty of complacency and compromise when it comes to my walk with the Lord and not diligently seeking and spending time with Him. I have also gotten wrapped up in making a living and trying to prosper in my own natural efforts and abilities.

I am not saying that God does not want his children to prosper, but we forget that prosperity comes from the Lord. Matthew 6 is very clear, *"But seek ye first the kingdom of God and His righteousness and all these things shall be added unto you."*

I don't think many Christians realize they are living under the curse. Christ set us free at Calvary, but we have returned to our bondage and enslavement. If you read the Exodus story, over and over Moses pleaded with Pharaoh to let the Israelites go into the desert to worship God. Pharaoh agreed to do so several times, but it says that God hardened his heart and he later refused.

But read Exodus 5 closely to see what Pharaoh did in the meantime:

Afterward, Moses and Aaron went to Pharaoh and said,
"This is what the Lord, the God of Israel, says: 'Let my people go, so that they may hold a festival to me in the wilderness.'"

2 Pharaoh said, "Who is the Lord, that I should obey him and let Israel go? I do not know the Lord and I will not let Israel go."

3 Then they said, "The God of the Hebrews has met with us. Now let us take a three-day journey into the wilderness to offer sacrifices to the Lord our God, or He may strike us with plagues or with the sword."

4 But the king of Egypt said, "Moses and Aaron, why are you taking the people away from their labor? Get back to your work!" 5 Then Pharaoh said, "Look, the people of the land are now numerous, and you are stopping them from working."

6 That same day Pharaoh gave this order to the slave drivers and overseers in charge of the people: 7 "You are no longer to supply the people with straw for making bricks; let them go and gather their own straw. 8 But require them to make the same number of bricks as before; don't reduce the quota. They are lazy; that is why they are crying out, 'Let us go and sacrifice to our God.' 9 Make the work harder for the people so that they keep working and pay no attention to lies."

Then the slave drivers and the overseers went out and said to the people, "This is what Pharaoh says: 'I will not give you any more straw. Go and get your own straw wherever you can find it, but your work will not be reduced at all.'"

So, the people scattered all over Egypt to gather stubble to use for straw. The slave drivers kept pressing them, saying, "Complete the work required of you for each day, just as when you had straw." And Pharaoh's slave drivers beat the Israelite overseers they had appointed, demanding, "Why haven't you met your quota of bricks yesterday or today, as before?"

Then the Israelite overseers went and appealed to Pharaoh: "Why have you treated your servants this way? Your servants are given no straw, yet we are told, 'Make bricks!' Your servants are being beaten, but the fault is with your own people."

Pharaoh said, "Lazy, that's what you are—lazy! That is why you keep saying, 'Let us go and sacrifice to the Lord.' Now get to work. You will not be given any straw, yet you must produce your full quota of bricks."

The Israelite overseers realized they were in trouble when they were told, "You are not to reduce the number of bricks required of you for each day." When they left Pharaoh, they found Moses and Aaron waiting to meet them, and they said, "May the Lord look on you and judge you! You have made us obnoxious to Pharaoh and his officials and have put a sword in their hand to kill us."

We were made to fellowship with God. From Genesis, we know that Adam and Eve spent time with God in the garden. Before the fall, they did not have to labor and work for their food.

God provided everything that they would need; however, after they ate the forbidden fruit, God told Adam, *"Because you listened to your wife and ate from the tree about which I commanded you, 'You must not eat of it,'* "Cursed is the ground because of you; through painful toil you will eat of it all the days of your life…By the sweat of your brow, you will eat your food until you return to the ground since from it you were taken…"

When Pharaoh told the Israelites that they now had to produce brick without straw, he was further enforcing the curse: work and toil.

Do you realize that many Christians are still living under this curse even though Jesus died to abolish it when we live in Him? Instead of trusting God for what we need, we work countless hours to either prosper or make ends meet, but what are we sacrificing? FELLOWSHIP WITH GOD!

Do you understand that the enemy wants to keep us so busy that we sever our lifeline with God? Haven't you noticed that we seem to work more but get paid less? Our standard of living continues to decline even though many of us are putting in longer hours. This is not by accident. This is by design. If satan can keep us out of the presence of God, he has us under his power and control.

We may go to church each week out of habit or to sing a few praises, but most of us are powerless when it comes to living a supernatural life in Christ. If we've sown carnal seeds how can we expect to reap a spiritual harvest? In these last days and hours, we must draw closer to God so that we can hear and recognize His voice and escape what is to come upon the earth.

Matthew 24:24 declares, *"For there shall arise false Christ's, and false prophets, and shall shew great signs and wonders; insomuch that, if it were possible, they shall deceive the very elect."*

Brothers and Sisters in Christ, it is time that we wake up and return to the Lord with our whole hearts so that the coming of the Lord does not approach us like a thief in the night.

All ten virgins in Matthew 25, were awaiting the Lord's return but all were not prepared when He arrived. Perhaps they were too bogged down with the affairs of life to pay attention to the signs.

Some Christian scholars suggest that the oil in their lamps signified the Holy Spirit. Could it be that there was no oil (Holy Spirit) in their lamps because they were not continually cultivating a growing and intimate relationship with God?

For God to live and move and have our being, we must unite with Him. We must become one, just as Jesus said, "I and the Father are one. " - St. John 10:30

Ask yourself today, where is your treasure? For where your treasure is, there goes your heart and attention. If you want to draw closer to God, you must spend time with Him. Is it time for you to return to your first love? I believe having a date with God can point you in the right direction or at least give you a jumpstart if you've been neglectful in spending time with God and growing intimately in love with Him.

Treacherous times are soon coming upon the earth and if we are not filled with God's power, faith, presence, anointing, and His Word, how are we going to survive? Whether you believe in a no, pre, mid, or post tribulation, it is possible that the church will all face horrendous trials. Just look at the Middle East, and the Christians who are being persecuted for following Christ. By God's mercy, we have escaped such conditions but that doesn't mean we always will.

I want the power of God living inside of me so I can endure, and live or even die for the cause of Christ. Being ready is so much more than just going to church and speaking Christian jargon.

Jesus said in Mark 16, "These signs will follow those who believe:

> *And these signs shall follow them that believe; In my name shall they cast out devils; they shall speak with new tongues; They shall take up serpents; and if they drink any deadly thing, it shall not hurt them; they shall lay hands on the sick, and they shall recover.*

This is the kind of faith we are going to need in the last days and the time to prepare is now!

Journaling- Write it Out:

1. Where really do your treasures lie?

2. What in your life is bogging you down and keeping you from spending time with God?

_____

_____

_____

3. Do you sometimes feel as if you've lost your first love? Why?

_____

_____

_____

_____

4. Think about some areas you can let go of that would provide more time to fellowship with God? What are they?

_____

_____

_____

_____

Closing Prayer:

Father God, I know it's so easy to get bogged down by busyness and the cares of this world and neglect intimate time with you. Renew my mind and help me to seek you first and foremost. I surrender all my "doing" unto you. Thank you for helping me prioritize my day by putting you first. I declare today that I will no longer operate under the curse, as you, through Christ, have set me free. Amen.

Put on the Full Armor of God

Ephesians 6: 10-17 –*"Finally, be strong in the Lord and in his mighty power. Put on the full armor of God, so that you can take your stand against the devil's schemes. For our struggle is not against flesh and blood, but against the rulers, against the authorities, against the powers of this dark world and against the spiritual forces of evil in the heavenly realms. Therefore, put on the full armor of God, so that when the day of evil comes, you may be able to stand your ground, and after you have done everything, to stand. Stand firm then, with the belt of truth buckled around your waist, with the breastplate of righteousness in place, and with your feet fitted with the readiness that comes from the gospel of peace. In addition to all this, take up the shield of faith, with which you can extinguish all the flaming arrows of the evil one. Take the helmet of salvation and the sword of the Spirit, which is the word of God."*

2 Corinthians 10:4-5 – *"For the weapons of our warfare are not carnal but mighty in God for pulling down strongholds, 5 casting down arguments and every high thing that exalts itself against the knowledge of God, bringing every thought into captivity to the obedience of Christ…"*

We as Christians are in a spiritual battle and if we want to win the fight, we must do so according to the kingdom of God. The scriptures above tell us that our fight is not carnal or of the flesh. We are fighting against demons and powers of evil in high places. We are fighting a battle that we cannot see with our natural eyes. When bad things happen, we often attribute them to bad luck or misfortunate, but behind the scene, spiritual warfare or an attack might be taking place. Too often we try to fight our battles from an earthly plane: getting angry with someone, yelling, being rude, or worse. Yet these are all characteristics of satan.

James 1:20 declares: *"Everyone should be quick to listen, slow to speak and slow to become angry because human anger does not produce the righteousness that God desires."*

If we want to win the fight, we must use God's weapons. This begins with putting on His Armor. God's armor includes truth (reality), righteousness (right-standing with God), peace (that passes all understanding), faith (unwavering), and the sword of the Spirit (God's Word). With these, we cast down erroneous thoughts and imaginations, declare God's Word over our circumstances, walk-in uprightness and truth, and stand in faith with peace until we see the victory.

You can use your date with God to empower you with God's armor so that you are always covered and prepared to take on the enemy throughout the day. Always remember the battle is fought with our mouths and on our knees through prayer.

2 Chronicles 7:14 declares, *"If my people, who are called by my name, will humble themselves and pray and seek my face and turn from their wicked ways, then I will hear from heaven, and I will forgive their sin and will heal their land."*

If we want to see real transformation in our lives, this is where it begins- seeking God's face through prayer, repentance, reading His Word, and spending time with Him.

So often, the real battle we most often fight is our own complacency and apathy when it comes to seeking God with our whole heart, soul, and strength. I hope having a date with God will give you the tools to seek God more consistently.

I believe we are not really in the true fight until we have stepped onto God's battlefield and are doing the works of God through the Holy Spirit. When we are truly about God's business, that's when the enemy will begin to strike, but greater is he that is in us, than he who is in the world. There is no need to fear when we have been fitted with God's armor.

Journaling- Write it Out:

1. In what ways have you been fighting your battles?

   _____

   _____

   _____

   _____

2. How has that worked in your life?

   _____

   _____

   _____

_____

3. Why must we fight the enemy with the weapons of God?

_____

_____

_____

_____

4. What are those weapons?

_____

_____

_____

_____

Closing Prayer:

Father God, today I make a declaration to stand in your power working within me. I am not defeated but a conqueror in Christ who loves and strengthens me. Today I put on the full armor of God: faith, love, and truth. I declare your word, the sword of the Spirit, above all other voices. Through speaking your word over my life and all situations, I shall destroy the attacks of the enemy in my life. Amen.

What Can I Expect from Pursuing God?

*"You will seek Me and find Me when you search for Me with all your heart." –
Jeremiah 29:13*

Many believers don't really know God. Please don't get offended when I say
this. I didn't, for many, many years. Although I had accepted Jesus Christ as my
personal Lord and Savior at 18-years-old, my relationship with God mostly
encompassed a lot of church services and activity. Instead of pursuing a thriving
and intimate relationship with God on my own, I tried to serve God by doing good
works. Even though I was serving Christ the best way I knew how, I still felt it
was not enough. One day, many years later, I began to ask myself, "At what point
would God be pleased with me? How much did I have to do to earn his love?" I
believe these questions started the process of my deliverance from works to
accepting God's free gift of grace. Finally, I embraced the fact that God does not
accept us based upon what we do, but upon our faith and trust in Him. I was set
free.

Just like me, many believers have adopted a church relationship with God.
They have never experienced, or at least consistently, the transformative power
and nature of God living in and through them. It's much like what Job described
in Job 42:5, *"My ears had heard of You but now my eyes have seen You."*

Jesus, through the power of the Holy Spirit, wants to live in you and through
you. God wants to use you for His kingdom and His glory. He literally wants to
change your life.

I believe so many Christians, especially in America, are depressed, joyless,
and feel they have no purpose because they continue to participate on the
sidelines, when their spirit is yearning and craving for more. It's craving the
greater things of God. But, instead, we settle for temporal security, mediocrity,
possessions, and pursuing the creation instead of the creator.

We've become like the rich young ruler who turned from God when asked to
give up all he had to follow Christ, not realizing that this was the very thing his
soul desired. Too often we allow fear and uncertainty to hold us back.

As you begin to abide in God's presence, nothing may happen at first. It
depends on your faithfulness and your consistency. It depends on how badly you
want it. God is seeking those who are seeking Him in Spirit as well as truth (John
4:23-24).

However, from my experience, and that of many others, if you continue to pursue God, your life WILL change. God will become more real to you than ever before. He will talk to you. He will fellowship with you. He will lead and guide you. He will fill your heart with an overflow of His love, joy, peace, purpose, and contentment.

Many of us have gotten it all wrong. We pursue God for what we can get: material and tangible blessings, comfort and prosperity, and security in this life. But the real question remains, are you truly happy? Are these things really satisfying your soul? If you're honest, probably not.

We believe the reward is in the blessings, but the REAL reward is Jesus Himself. The ultimate reward is Jesus. The goal of our life shouldn't be more blessings or more stuff. The goal is knowing, fellowshipping, and being loved by Jesus, the creator of the universe, for in *"His presence is fullness of joy and at His right hand there are pleasures evermore."* (Psalm 16:11).

Whether you realize it or not, your soul is seeking the love, joy, peace, and purpose that only a rich, growing, and intimate relationship with God can provide. Nothing else can fulfill this deepest human desire.

In closing, I want to read you a slightly altered version of 2 Chronicles 7:14, that if My people, who are called by My name, will humble themselves and pray and seek My face and turn from their secular ways, then I will hear from heaven and I will forgive their sins and heal their land (their marriages, relationships, families, community).

If you want to pursue Jesus, join the movement to get one million believers seeking after God with all their heart, soul, and strength. A date with God will get you on your way.

Journaling- Write it Out:

1. Are you satisfied with your relationship with God? Why or why not?

_____

_____

_____

2. What do you feel is missing from your relationship with God?

_____

_____

_____

_____

3. Why are you ready to seek God now with all your heart, soul, and strength?

_____

_____

_____

_____

Closing Prayer:

Father God, I'm so excited that there is more I can attain by seeking you first. I don't just want a church or sometime relationship with you. I want to know you fully and become one with you, just as you are one with Christ. Father, I ask today that you reveal yourself to me more and more, as I dwell in your presence and surrender my heart to you. Amen.

Why Meditate?

Can abiding in God's presence and meditating on God, His Word, and His character really benefit your life and walk with the Messiah? Absolutely! In this lesson, you'll discover the transformative power of Christian meditation and its many benefits. Maintaining a regular Christian meditation practice can improve your life as well and your relationship with God. Through consistent meditation you will:

Enjoy greater peace of mind by eliminating worrisome and negative thoughts.

The scriptures tell us to cast down every thought and imagination that exalts itself against the knowledge of God. The problem is that many believers have chronically negative thought lives that they may not even be aware of and that may be contributing to depression, anxiety, and other toxic emotions. Through Biblical meditation, you will become the observer of your mental chatter and learn how to cast down or eliminate destructive or negative thinking and replace them with God's Word.

Create more balance to carry out your values and nurture your whole self.

Busyness is not an attribute of the Most High. We create a hectic lifestyle when we try to accomplish more than we are mentally and physically capable. Even just stepping off the treadmill of life can be extremely daunting. When we're so used to striving and struggling, we miss out on the opportunity to gain greater balance and make decisions not based upon urgency, but on the values and yearnings of our own heart. Christian meditation creates that space we need to stop and listen to God and ourselves. God tells us to honor the Sabbath and keep it holy. What better way than to incorporate a regular time with God and a Biblical meditation practice.

Develop a greater sensitivity to the Holy Spirit and learn to discern His voice, leading, and promptings.

Our Savior often speaks to His children in a still small voice through impressions, promptings, inspiration, and circumstances. However, if we're too distracted to listen or our lives are filled with constant noise and activity, we can miss out on important messages from Him.

Biblical meditation creates quiet moments that give the Holy Spirit room to speak to us and gives us the divine guidance we need to navigate successfully through life.

Live with more joy and contentment WITHOUT changing your circumstances.

1 Timothy 6:6-8 declares, *"But Godliness with contentment is great gain, for we brought nothing into the world, and we cannot take anything out of the world."* Do you find yourself seeking after the things of this world for peace, joy, or contentment? If so, you are not alone. The enemy has deceived believers and unbelievers alike that happiness is acquired by obtaining material goods, relationships, and things outside of God's Kingdom. But nothing could be farther from the truth. Peace, joy, and contentment come from abiding and trusting in God. When we enter into God's Presence something supernatural happens. We can't "be with God" and not be changed. Little by little the rudiments of this world begin to dissolve, and we are able to walk in God's peace and joy WITHOUT any changes to our circumstances.

Alleviate stress and other stress-related illnesses.

In recent years, the interest in various forms of meditation have skyrocketed with doctors, celebrities, and health professionals touting the many mental and physical benefits of a regular meditation practice. In addition, studies have proven that it's true. If you need a free and quick way to reduce stress, look no further. What makes Biblical meditation even more beneficial is that you're meditating on God's Word with the intention of experiencing His manifesting presence.

Develop greater intimacy with God and increased wisdom.

The Bible says that when we draw close to God that He draws closer to us. The Most High said, *"You will seek me and find me when you search for me with all your heart."* Many believers don't make intimacy with God a priority. They think that going to church and hearing a sermon is all they need to do to fulfill their Biblical duty. The fact you're reading this journal means that you're looking for more than just a church or surface relationship with God. You most likely want to know and experience God in a deeper and more intimate way.

As you spend time with God just abiding with Him and meditating on His Word, you are literally transformed, and God's Presence will become more real to you than ever before. Our Savior said in Matthew that we can't put new wine (thoughts) into old wine bottles (mind-sets) without corrupting the old batch. If we are to fully embrace the Scriptures, we must pull up the weeds of doubt, fear, and unbelief.

Bring Your Flesh under the Authority of the Christ

Sometimes we just need to say NO to our flesh, but that can be difficult if it has been holding the reins for so long. Unwanted habits and addictions, even chronic negativity, are all signs that your flesh may be out of control. Subduing the flesh first begins with subduing the mind and its impulsive thoughts that often play like a background record in our subconscious mind. Your thoughts have created your current reality because thoughts are things. The longer we meditate on specific circumstances (whether good or bad) the quicker they come into fruition. Biblical meditation can help you bring your flesh under subjection as you learn to notice, release, and then eliminate or replace compulsive thinking with God's Word.

"Christian meditation allows you to take the reins and direct your own thoughts back where they belong: under the authority of the Savior and His Word."

Journaling- Write it Out:

1. What have been your thoughts about meditation before starting this journal?

_____

_____

_____

_____

2. Which of the benefits would you like to glean from Christian meditation?

_____

_____

_____

_____

3. Can you think of any scriptures regarding meditation? If not, consider doing a search on this subject.

_____

_____

_____

_____

Closing Prayer:

Heavenly Father, I can see that there are many benefits to Christian meditation. I am so grateful to be introduced to this practice that can transform my life as well as deepen my relationship with you. I know it is no accident that I am reading this meditation journal. You desire to have an intimate relationship with me and all of your children. I am excited about where this spiritual journey will lead me. Amen.

Living in Alignment with God & Your Purpose # 1

This has become my new mantra: living in alignment with God. It sounds so simple, but just like meditation, it has its challenges. Living in alignment with God means that God is always in the driver's seat and that we are doing things God's way and in His timing. Living out of alignment with God means that we are in the driver's seat and trying to control all or most aspects of our lives. One brings joy and bliss, the other frustration, fear, and disillusion.

So how do you know when you are living in alignment with God? Easy, you feel at peace, full of joy, and sometimes blissful. You love your life and what you are doing, and that doesn't need to be anything major or grand. However, you wake up each day excited and glad to be alive.

This by no way means you won't have challenges, encounter setbacks, or have your bad days. Yet, when living in alignment with God, you quickly turn these things over to God because He's the boss and He's the one to figure it out and carry the heavy loads. It's a matter of casting all your cares upon Him because He cares for you.

Whatever you need, you ask God to provide it in the best way He sees fit. Many times, we try to make things happen in our own way or efforts, and we don't get the results we want. Or if we do, we then set a precedent for having to "do it ourselves" in order to maintain success.

It's really an "outcome" and "destination" based way of living. However, I have found on my own spiritual journey that it's not the destination that I'm really after. No, I want joy, peace, and passion in my life right now and that comes from doing what makes me feel good and inspired every day. For me, that is writing and creating! I could write all day long and do nothing else, I love it that much. So, I make sure that I incorporate lots of it in my life.

For you it could be time spent with your children; however, trying to reach some future destination may have relegated this joyful experience to the back burner so you can reach your goals, with lots of stress, anxiety, and frustration to boot.

Or maybe you are a business owner who works 24-7. Your body may not be at work all this time, but your mind is. You're constantly thinking of marketing or ways to get ahead, but no matter what you do, it feels like you're spinning your wheels and that doesn't feel good. You're probably out of alignment, using too much of your own intellect to get things done or reach a destination that you "think" will bring you happiness, security, or satisfaction. That is nothing more than an illusion.

Instead, focus on drawing closer to God, asking God to provide what you need, and then just enjoy the ride. Do what you love most and what brings you the most joy. That's what I started doing and it changed my life. I know that running a business takes more than just doing the fun stuff, but the fun stuff is what makes life fun and rewarding.

I may need to relegate the stuff I don't like too much to others, but mostly, I want to experience joy every day and not just when I make a certain amount of money. If you can't enjoy your life with beans and rice, you won't enjoy it with a daily diet of steak and potatoes either. Joy comes from within, by embracing the things that matter most, and following your heart and not your head.

That's one way we know we're out of alignment with God, we feel it in our bodies as well as our emotions. We're not happy, not complete, and say things like, "Is this really what life is all about," or "I need to change; I need to do something different, something that makes me happy and brings me joy."

Living in alignment also means allowing God to live in you and through you. We are the TEMPLE of the Holy Spirit, a vessel for God to dwell within. When we are in alignment, we can feel God's presence within us, kind of like what you experience during meditation. Your whole body feels energized and you could stay in that state forever; if you didn't have chores and other natural things to do. Or sometimes you've felt God inside of you during a worship service while you were praising and giving Him glory.

I'm not saying that every minute of the day we should be on a holy high, but we should do our best to stay in alignment with God so he can "direct our paths," and we can feel His presence.

You might be thinking, "Yes" I want this, but I have no idea how to bring it about in my life. Your meditation practice and the spiritual disciplines in this book will help you with that. The more time you spend in God's presence through meditation, the easier it will be to decipher the invisible world inside you as well as around you. You will notice the subtle differences in feeling God's peace versus feeling anxiety, fear, or irritation. All of these are internal guidance systems to let you know when, you are or aren't in alignment with God.

Being out of alignment with God is really a form of fear. Fear of lack is usually behind our desire to control. When it comes to lack, many fear the lack of finances, purpose, youth, beauty, success, failure, and more. Whenever we feel a sense of lack, we try to compensate for it, meaning, we get out of alignment with God and try to meet our needs in our own way.

When doing this, we're not being motivated by love, light, and God, but by fear and "fear brings torment." That's why we can't be truly happy or in bliss when we're operating in fear; instead we feel urgency, frustration, and stress. Instead, we must put our needs, wants, and desires on God's to-do list and we wait for Him to guide us or outright bless us instead.

If you feel you lack money (or whatever), when you are in alignment and trusting God, you might say to God, Lord you know I need more money for this or that, I don't know how you are going to supply it but I'm trusting you. From here, we stay in tune with the Holy Spirit that will lead us and guide us into all truth. We stay open to opportunities and we listen to our hearts and not our heads. God will bring us what we need when we need it. We don't have to be as the Gentiles and worry about it and take matters into our own hands.

When we are in fear, we begin to worry, and this creates stress. Then we try to find ways to meet our needs like searching desperately online for ways to make money fast, take a second job that totally burns us out and limits our time for what really matters.

As I said, this is so much easier said than done. We must die daily to our fears and let God move into the driver's seat. Your daily meditation practice will help you to keep God at the forefront of your life as well as gain greater sensitivity so you can stay in alignment with God and His leadings.

Inviting God In

I want to encourage you to invite God into whatever you are facing. Whether it is pain or hurt, a crisis, a bad situation, or even uncomfortable emotions, God is available to see you through. When we invite God in, we are infusing our suffering with His light and darkness must flee. Sometimes during my meditation time, when a thought or worry surfaces, instead of detaching from it or pushing it away, I will invite God into it right then and there and then return to my sacred word, scripture, or my breath.

For example, if I am meditating and thoughts about "the squirrels eating my tomatoes" pops into my head, I may pause and silently say, "Father God, help me to figure out how to keep the squirrel away from my tomatoes." Or I may have thoughts about "book marketing," and think "Father God, thank you for guiding my book marketing efforts step-by-step."

Inviting God into our thoughts, decisions, and even our pain gives Him permission to work for us and even start the healing process. By acknowledging thoughts and emotions, we bring awareness to them, and that is the first step to both solutions and healing. When we're living in alignment with God, we don't want our solutions but God's, because we know that God knows us and what we need to be content. He also knows and sees everything. He knows what we need before we even ask, but asking gets the ball rolling for us. Jesus said, "You have not because you ask not, "so use every opportunity to get God working on your behalf, then rest and trust that He will. For without faith it is impossible to please God and *"we walk by faith and not by sight."*

Journaling- Write it out?

1. How do we know when we're living in alignment with God?

_____

_____

_____

_____

2. How do we know when we're NOT living in alignment with God?

_____

_____

_____

_____

3. What fears may be holding you back from really trusting God and giving Him all of you?

_____

_____

_____

_____

4. What is a situation you are facing right now that you can invite in God's love, healing, and light?

_____

_____

_____

_____

Closing Prayer:

Father God, I desired to live in alignment with you. I want to experience, daily, the joy, peace, and contentment I'm enjoying in my life right now and not at some future moment. I also invite you into all I am struggling with or facing. Thank you for bringing your light and healing. I commit to trusting and resting in you. Amen.

13 Steps to Living in Alignment with God & Your Purpose # 2

Below are some steps to follow to begin to live in alignment with God and your purpose:

1. Ask for guidance

If you're committed to living in alignment with God and your life purpose, ask for guidance, clarity, and help/assistance. According to Mathew 7:7-8, *"Ask, and it shall be given; knock and it shall be opened; seek and you'll find."*

Therefore, continually ask God for what you need and desire. In addition, ask God for help, strength, wisdom, guidance, confidence, and to reveal to you the paths you are meant to take. Be confident that He will reveal to you all the hidden treasures, gifts, and talents within you as you draw closer to Him in faith, trust, and patience.

2. Move on from your past lessons.

It's important that we bring every thought captive in an effort to renew our minds and eliminate those thoughts that cripple our lives. Too many of us live in the past, reliving old wounds, and playing them over and over again like a broken record. Sometimes this requires inner healing; other times, we just need to focus on eliminating toxic thoughts and rewriting our mental scripts. Want to be truly free, move on from your past mistakes and failures or stop burying or denying them, and allow healing to take place. (You'll learn some techniques later on.) Learn from the lessons of your past, forgive yourself and others, and know that God is still working all things together for your highest good, no matter how badly you messed up.

3. Get out of the driver's seat.

Your mind is limited, but not your heart. For this reason, it's important to move beyond thoughts alone and listen to the still small voice from within. That's God talking to you! To do this, we often must let go of fixed plans and ideas, allowing ourselves to be open to new possibilities and directions.

The heart knows what you need. Even God said, "I know what you need before you even ask." When we rely solely on our minds, we can't see past our limitations and fears. When we follow our heart and live in alignment with God, it will take you to places you've never even dreamed of, as well as reveal to you things you've never even thought were possible.

Also, don't worry about how or when things will happen in your life. Your only requirement is to trust God one day at a time and be responsive to His leadings. Let God work out all the details for you. Get rid of your time frames. You want God's best in His timing and when you're prepared to receive. The Bible says that God will "add unto" us. Unfortunately, too often we try to get it for ourselves. Not only does that bring frustration and a lot of striving, we never get the peace and fulfillment of receiving from God. That doesn't mean work won't be involved, but when we trust God, we know our work will be fruitful and never in vain. We can spend years trying to obtain what God can bless us with, in just one hour. Just have fun fishing (living your best life) and cast down your net when and where God tells you to. Then you reap enough to share with others.

4. Move on from your old life.

Jesus said I came that they might have life and have it more abundantly. Although many of us aren't really satisfied with our lives, we have a difficult time making the necessary changes to obtain the life we truly want. Part of this is due to ignorance as well as fear. It's hard moving from certainty to uncertainty or from comfort to taking risks. Instead, we rather keep everything the same. When we begin to live our life in alignment with God, we must trust that He loves us enough to give us the very best, and in reality, many of us don't really know what that is. We've gotten our cues from advertisements and the media as to what's important to be happy. Yet, our discontentment continues to grow. When we decide to really turn our lives over to God, it requires holding God's hands (really tightly) and allowing Him to guide us. His best for us includes joy, contentment, and fulfillment, in other words, a more abundant life.

Once you make this commitment, chances are you'll feel as though the rug has been pulled from beneath your feet, like a free fall. As you move forward, you'll notice many things such as past beliefs, places, experiences, and relationships that were not matching up with your life purpose begin to fall away.

This is making room for new, better and healthier events to unfold. If this happens, don't be surprised; instead, see it as part of the cleansing, renewal, and regeneration process that you need to go through to get into alignment with God and your purpose.

5. Prepare to go through some darkness

Speaking of being uncomfortable, expect some unexpected drama to show up as you move into true alignment with God and your purpose. Sometimes this drama will be created by you – either consciously or unconsciously, or by those around you. Instead of getting into fear, remember that this is all happening for your own growth and evolution. As you let go of your old ways of being, there is a type of dying to the self or the ego, as its power over you diminishes. The ego doesn't want to go or give up its authority without a fight. Keep your eyes on Jesus and know that this too shall pass. From the darkness shall emerge God's glorious light and you will be changed for the better.

6. Drop your ego

Paul in the Bible said, *"I die daily."* What he meant is that every day he laid his ego down to follow the ways of God and Spirit. In order to live in alignment with God and your purpose, you must begin to think differently.

This is the time to detach from your own perceptions of how life should be, or people should behave. In addition, let go of your likes and dislikes, which keep you in bondage from experiencing anything outside of your box. Instead, begin to see life as a playground to explore by surrendering to what is and what shows up in your life. Begin to walk by faith and not by sight. Trust in unseen things as well as God's spirit living inside of you. In the days ahead, you'll be quieting the incessant chatter of the ego, which is parading itself as your thoughts. Quiet its voice and connect to your inner knowing more often.

7. Look at life from a different perspective

Being fully aligned with your heart's purpose has nothing to do with fortune, fame, power, and recognition, but all about living a life of joy, peace, love, and being of service. It's about offering the work inside your heart and sharing all of your God-given gifts and talents with others. Make decisions based upon what feels right and that will bring you joy.

When you are operating from love and bliss, life always has a way of looking after you, and for anything that you give, God will return it back to you tenfold.

According to Wayne Dyer, an American motivational speaker, and self-help author, you'll never have enough if you chase after money.

Instead, focus on living each day with joy, peace, and purpose, then every day is a reward in itself.

8. Welcome the many gifts of life with open arms.

As you begin to live a more heart-centered life, by reprogramming your mind and being led by the Holy Spirit instead of your head, your whole life will fall into alignment. New doors of opportunity may open up for you, new experiences will present themselves, and even new people will come into your life. These are all showing up to assist you in your new journey. Don't discount anything that happen. Ask God what you should do with this information and then listen to the still small voice in your heart. Don't judge, as you never know the end results of any situation or circumstance. With God at the helm, many of the solutions or desires we seek are off our visual and mental radar. God's ways are not our ways, nor His thoughts our thoughts.

Try to welcome all that life offers you with open arms, as you never know what life's gifts have in store for you. They're all meant to help you fulfill the meaningful and beautiful work you're supposed to do in life.

9. Always show gratitude.

For every interaction and experience you encounter, whether perceived as either good or bad, always show your gratitude and appreciation. The Bible even tells us to give thanks in all things as you never know what blessings can arise even from your discomfort or pain.

Let life know that you're always grateful for the numerous and precious gifts it keeps blessing you with. And yes, the more you appreciate the life you're currently living, the more life will give you reasons to be thankful. According to Meister Eckhart, a German theologian and philosopher, only saying a prayer of thank you in your entire life can be enough.

10. Always have faith.

As you move towards being in alignment with God and your purpose, you will eventually discover that you're on what Jesus called, "the narrow" path. Many Christians think this passage refers to hell, but instead, I believe it's referring to those who are truly seeking to know and experience God, are few and far between. Yes, many people have a church experience, but not many are living in alignment with God.

You might also discover that few people understand your new way of being and you may start to feel alone and misunderstood sometimes. If this happens, it's very easy to begin doubting yourself and your decisions. This is normal. Try to keep in mind that people who aren't living in alignment with God and their purpose can't understand those who are, so don't let this deter you. Gain whatever strength and encouragement you need from God alone. Go frequently into your secret place (time of meditation and God's presence) to wash away the fears and doubt of others.

Ralph Waldo Emerson, an American essayist concluded that to be great you must be misunderstood because even Jesus, Galileo, Copernicus, Luther, Socrates, Pythagoras, and Newton were all misunderstood despite being pure and wise.

11. Be soft like water.

To be soft like water means that you go with the flow of the Spirit. When you encounter rocks, logs, or obstacles in your path, you gently move around or through them instead of fighting and kicking to move them out of your way. Do things and travel to places that are calling you inwardly and trust your inner wisdom. Sometimes God will lead you out of your comfort zone, just to show you that you "can" do it. Growth is always at the end of our fear.

Simply follow life's natural rhythm and share your inner light and presence, as well as your work, and love with everyone around you. Let go of all your attachments, those things that weigh you down, and just be.

12. Seek inner peace.

By aligning yourself more fully with God, you'll begin to feel a deep sense of tranquility and inner peace. Feelings of fear, frustration, anxiety, and doubt are all signals that, you've veered off your life's path, either physically or mentally.

Let peace, joy, and bliss pull you along. Jesus said that we can have peace that passes all understanding. Your meditation practice will help you to quiet as well as renew your mind.

This inner peace and calm will make it easier for you to hear your inner voice as well as follow your heart and soul's wise advice.

13. Embrace humility.

As you begin to notice all sorts of wonderful and amazing things happening in your life, you might be tempted to think that you're better than those around you. However, it's just your ego trying hard to separate you from everyone else. Just remain humble and embrace humility because this will only make God's voice become clearer and louder.

Furthermore, humility strengthens your soul, whereas pride and arrogance can only weaken it. When you're deeply aligned and connected with God and your purpose, you'll start recognizing yourself in all things and people. This's because your heart is full of love and compassion for both yourself and those around you.

Journal – Write it Out:

1. Is your life in alignment with God and your purpose? Explain…

_____

_____

_____

_____

2. What resonated with you most about living your life in alignment with God?

_____

_____

_____

_____

3. What do you think living in alignment with one's life purpose means for you?

_____

_____

_____

_____

4. Do you think each one of us have a specific purpose to fulfill in life? Explain…

_____

_____

_____

_____

5. What can you start doing today, to begin to align yourself with God?

_____

_____

_____

_____

Closing Prayer:

Father God, I desire to live in alignment with you and your purpose. Living in alignment with you means surrendering to the Spirit by relinquishing control. "For I know the plans I have for you," says God, "to give you hope and a future." I believe there is no better place to be than on the narrow path with you. Thank you today for taking the reins and leading me, moment by moment, in action and being. Amen.

the
basics

The Basics

Day 1:
Getting Started

In this section, you will learn how to turn your quiet time into a daily hour of power one step and day at a time. Each day you will be introduced to spiritual disciplines that will help you to build the right quiet time for you according to your needs, desires, interests, and time. You will not only learn how to meditate, but how to create a quiet time that will draw you closer to God, help you make your dreams become a reality, and live with more peace and joy by working through your limiting beliefs, negative thoughts, and toxic emotions.

My time with God can last anywhere from 15 minutes to 2 hours if I have the extra time and really need to work through some emotional blocks, but it's well worth it to me. I always try to leave my date with God feeling free, refreshed, and at peace. Presently, I do my date with God first thing in the morning or just before I retire.

By spending time in the morning, you're most receptive to the Holy Spirit and can start your day centered in the Lord. However, if you just can't find the time in the morning due to work and other obligations, spending time with God in the evening can be just as rewarding.

For years, when my children were younger and lived at home, I spent time with God in the evenings. After dinner and once everyone was settled in for the evening, I would make my way to my bedroom, lock the door, and just dwell in God's presence, sometimes for hours. I actually craved this time and looked forward to it, and I was never disappointed. It was as if God was there waiting for me as His sweet and loving Spirit permeated my room, body, and spirit.

I believe that once you get started, you will discover just how powerful these spiritual disciplines, tools, and activities can be to your spiritual, mental, and emotional health. I love spending time with God and working through many of the disciplines and activities you will learn because I always finish feeling lighter and more enthusiastic about my day. It is like a shower of the mind and my chance to begin my day, or end my day, without any of the residue of yesterday, last week, or even last year. Every day, I get to wipe the slate clean and start again feeling refreshed and renewed. Isn't that worth it? Is this the dying daily that Paul was talking about?

Isaiah 26:3 declares, *"You [God] will keep him in perfect peace, whose mind is stayed on You, because he trusts in You."*

If your heart is filled with worry and anxiety, it is a clear indication that your mind is not on the Lord. Instead of meditating on God and His promises, your eyes are on the news, the economy, or even your circumstances.

Whatever we meditate on becomes bigger in our focus. Therefore, stop dwelling on the problem and begin to put your attention on the solution (Jesus). By continually spending time with God and meditating on His promises, you'll quell your fearful thoughts, overshadow negative reports, and rise above your circumstances. Your date with God can strengthen and fortify your faith in Christ and build you up for when real disaster strikes.

One last reminder, this is YOUR time and you need to make it your way. These spiritual disciplines and schedules are only guidelines. You may want to switch things around a bit as you get deeper into the program, and that's okay; however, before you do, progress in the order presented to give yourself a chance to experience all the activities.

Also, you will notice that with each daily quiet time and activities I may list a time frame. Use this to help guide your time with God if you are under a crunch. If you ONLY have 15 minutes available, that's better than having no time at all. If you have more time, then just go with the flow of the Holy Spirit. You might also be wondering how you are supposed to fit this extra time in your already compacted schedule. You may just have to let something else go, maybe the television or some other activity. I also recommend going to bed an hour or two earlier so you can wake up earlier to get in your time with God.

In the meantime, start to look for a journal or notebook that you love. You will be spending a lot of time writing your inspirations, God's messages to you, and more.

Journaling- Write it Out:

1. How much time do you have to devote to your time with God each day?

_____

_____

_____

2. Will you spend that time in the morning or the evenings?

_____

_____

_____

_____

3. How will you help yourself to be consistent?

_____

_____

_____

_____

A few tips on being consistent:

Set a specific time each day and keep it. Add it to your day planner and see it as a valuable appointment with your spiritual CEO to help you begin your day with peace, guidance, and clarity.

Chunk routines together. For example, if you have a routine of drinking tea, exercising, or anything else, whether in the morning or evening, add your time with God to the mix. This will be a helpful reminder.

Keep your appointment even when you don't feel like it. That's your ego talking, and you don't want to listen. The more you "don't" want to keep your date with God is the time you need it most to subdue the flesh and keep your spirit in control.

We'll discuss these more in later lessons.

Day 2:
Set an Appointment with God

When you think about going on a date, you make arrangements with your date ahead of time. When you make a date, you keep it unless you let the other party know in advance. Your date with God is just as sacred. Setting a daily or weekly time for your date with God will go a long way in helping you to keep it. If you look at your date with God as something you do when you "feel" like it, the chances of keeping it will be slim. Without a commitment, there will always be some reason or urgency that will seem more important, but what could be more important than fellowshipping with the Lord. God desires our fellowship, and hopefully, by now, we know how important it is to our mental and spiritual well-being.

I think we sometimes believe we are doing God a favor by spending time with Him, but it is us that is really benefiting. Just think of your date with God as a daily deposit of love, joy, provision, miracles, strength, and guidance. The time you spend with God can take days, weeks, and years off of what you might be trying to accomplish on your own or in your own strength. Therefore, set a time and try to keep it. Make a solid decision not to let anything interfere with your date with God. If a daily appointment is not possible, then schedule what will work for you whether it is every morning, three times per week, the weekends, or your Sabbath day with the Lord. God honors the commitments that we make to Him. Also, I believe as you spend time with God, your desire to abide with Him will increase as you observe the benefits of his transformative presence and casting all your cares upon Him.

By now you might be thinking, okay, when will I start to meditate and "actually" spend time with God? You have started to develop a habit to prepare for your time with God. Each day you have learned more about the importance of spending time with God followed by some journaling questions and prayer to help you to internalize this information and your need for God even further. Everything that you have done so far to prepare is so important.

One thing I want you to always remember is that transformation takes time; therefore, it's always best to settle in and enjoy the journey. This book is designed to help you take those consistent baby-steps toward your goal of becoming a more spiritual Christian. Also, don't underestimate small beginnings. Every little bit you do can make a huge impact on your life. Even just 15 minutes per day, if you do it consistently, will get you great results. That's the key, patience, and consistency.

Think of your date with God as a part of your new lifestyle, something that will be a part of your day for years to come. By the time you finish this journal, you'll have lots of tools and knowledge to keep it going and create the date with God that works best for you for this time in your life.

Now it's time to schedule your time with God. We do this because we're more likely to keep our appointments if we write them down. If you have a daily or weekly planner, be sure and write your appointment in it and do your best not to miss it.

Below, schedule and then record your Date with God appointment below. Place a check and complete one or more)

_____ Daily from _____ to _____.

_____ Weekdays (Monday through Friday) from _____ to _____.

_____ Weekends (Saturdays and Sundays) from _____ to _____.

_____ On day(s) _____ from _____ to

_____.

Day 3:
Preparing to Meditate

If you're not aware of this already, Christian meditation is the foundation of *The Christian Meditation Journal,* so we're going to start there and here's why? One of the hardest things for us to do is to be still. Being able to control our thoughts and quiet our minds is essential to transforming every aspect of our lives. This week we're going to focus just on getting started with a daily meditation routine. I'm going to teach you several simple meditation techniques. Most of these have an accompanied guided audio as well.

In addition, if you only have 10-15 minutes of "God time" each day, start it with meditation. In my opinion, dwelling in God's presence, or Christian meditation, is the most important discipline of your time with God because it is the time that you purposefully enter into God's presence or secret place. It's the place where we cease from all our doing, to "just be" present with God.

During traditional devotionals, many Christians read their Bibles and pray, but rarely do they take the time to just dwell in God's presence. I feel this is one of the missing links in the church. I meet Christians constantly who are anxious, restless, angry, confused, and fearful.

They have never been taught the correlation between their thoughts, emotions, and behaviors. They continuously battle with depression, worry, anxiety, and other toxic emotions. They can recite God's Word left and right, but their inner spirit has never been washed and renewed. They have never become quiet long enough to consciously listen to their mental tape recorder and what it is playing. Or if they do, they quickly turn it off with outside distractions and noise.

Coming before the Lord in quietness and stillness is like entering the inner room of God. The Bible says that in God's *presence is the fullness of joy and no darkness can dwell there. John 1:15 says, "This is the message we have heard from Him and declare to you: God is light; in Him there is no darkness at all."* When we enter into God's presence, we are entering into His light. All darkness must flee. This is a supernatural phenomenon. God's transformative light changes us from the inside out and the more time we spend in His Presence, the more we are transformed into the image of God.

I believe we are uncomfortable with being still because we are afraid to face our inner demons. We're not sure what is going to surface in our thoughts. Often during times of stillness, forgotten hurts and pains from the past begin to creep up.

We may begin to remember things we want to deny or forget. When this happens, it can feel as though the walls are closing in on us. Fear may begin to arise in our hearts as we don't know what to do or how to deal with these thoughts, feelings, or images.

These blasts from the past don't surface to haunt you; they are trickling up because they want to set you free! They want to be released into the healing light and presence of God Almighty. God wants you to give all your cares and burdens to Him. He wants you to ask Him for forgiveness if needed, and then to let them go, but you can't give to God what you hide or deny.

Here is your chance to come clean and surrender all before the Lord. He knows it anyway and He wants to set you free. *"For whom the Son sets free, is free indeed."* We try so hard to change in our own effort, but that's not Biblical. If we could have changed by ourselves, Christ would not have had to die for us. No, God wants to change us. He is the Potter and we are the Clay. The only thing we need to do for change to happen is to submit ourselves to the Lord. By submission, we come into His Presence and sit at His feet. This is what happens during meditation. You submit yourself before the Lord and become completely bare and transparent before Him. Then He can do the work.

Meditation is also one of the best ways to root out restlessness by allowing the Holy Spirit within you to take authority over your whims and distractions. If you have a problem with being still, it is a clear indication that you are not in control. When it comes to dealing with issues, are you more reactive or proactive? Reactive behavior stems from a cluttered mind that doesn't have much room to think or contemplate before acting.

People who act proactively give space to their thoughts and then chose behaviors that will bring about the best outcome. Think of meditation as a practice to unravel your will (ego), strengthen your spirit, and to connect with God more spiritually.

If you will practice meditation daily, after a short while, you'll begin to look forward to and appreciate this quiet time with the Lord. Your day won't feel complete without it. Scripture or guided meditation gives God the opportunity to minister to you and allows you to just "be" with God, just how you are. In the beginning, it will probably be the hardest part of your date with God. Don't give into the urge to rush through it. That urge signifies your need for it even more.

In an upcoming lesson, we will start with a 10-minute meditation. In the meantime, I would like to invite you to check out some guided Christians available for free on my website or Daily Christian Meditations on my YouTube channel. Consider also downloading my Christian Meditator App (when available) to have access to over 60 guided meditation and affirmation recordings on a variety of topics. Currently, I use my listening library during my quiet times and it really comes in handy. Below are a few of my favorites.

Controlling Negative Thoughts
As I Open My Eyes
Pure Living Water Meditation
Jesus is my Healer Meditation

You don't have to do any of these now, but as you progress through the program, you may desire to use one of the guided meditations suggested above (or others) instead. Learning a basic meditation that you can do anywhere is important as you want to be able to meditate anytime and anyplace, whether on vacation, at home, or even in the park. For now, spend the first week with me practicing the simple meditation technique I will share tomorrow.

Journaling- Write it Out:

1. The last time I meditated I... Or, I have never meditated because ...

_____

_____

_____

_____

2. When I try to be still and spend time in silence, I feel...

_____

_____

_____

_____

3. What toxic thoughts or emotions would you like to wash away with
   meditation?

_____

_____

_____

_____

Day 4:
Invite God into Your Meditation Practice

"And whatever you do, whether in word or deed, do it all in the name of the Lord Jesus, giving thanks to God the Father through Him." – Colossian 3:17

Before meditating, I like to invite God and the Holy Spirit into my meditation practice with a short prayer. The Holy Spirit is our comforter and guide to all truth, and we need His help to connect with God in spirit and truth. When we meditate, we are entering more deeply into the spiritual realm. This invisible realm contains both heavenly angels as well as darker forces, but don't let that hinder you from meditating. These forces are everywhere whether we are meditating or not. If we want to worship God in spirit and truth, we've got to dive into the spiritual things of God, and meditation is one of them. We never have to fear darkness when we walk in the light. We walk in that light by keeping our hearts pure and living in alignment with God and our spirit. Let me make it clear, God never punishes us; however, when we dabble in unholy behaviors, we open the door to darkness in our lives. Praise God it only takes confession and turning away to get back on the right path.

"Therefore, confess your sins to each other and pray for each other so that you may be healed. The prayer of a righteous person is powerful and effective."- James 5:16

Confession cleanses the soul and brings healings. It's releasing and letting go of the poison that is pulling us away from operating in our divine nature. Father God wants us to be happy and whole, and that's impossible when we're carrying around guilt, burdens, or other weights.

Even Jesus told the disciples that before you come to the altar to pray and bring your gifts, if you have a problem with anyone, go to that person and get it right. Then come back and pray. God knows that when we are plagued with anger, heaviness, unforgiveness, or toxic thoughts and emotions, we can't give our best to Him.

Therefore, if you are offering your gift at the altar and there remember that your brother has something against you, leave your gift there before the altar. First, go and be reconciled to your brother, then come and offer your gift." -Matthew 5: 23-24

Your meditation practice is truly a gift to God because he loves when we spend time with Him, but it's really more for our benefit than His. When we become one with God and follow his Spirit, our lives will reap the blessings of inner peace, joy, and contentment.

> *If our hearts condemn us, we know that God is greater than our hearts, and He knows everything. Dear friends, if our hearts do not condemn us, we have confidence before God and receive from Him anything we ask because we keep His commands and do what pleases Him.* − 1 John 3:20-22

When our conscience is pure, we can come into the presence of God with boldness and confidence. The above scripture lets us know when we ask, we can receive anything from God when our hearts are pure and not condemning us. You know that gut feeling that you shouldn't have done or said that? Through prayer before meditation, it's a good idea to examine your heart to see if there is anything that might be standing in the way of your fellowship with God and receiving all He has for you. Keeping His commandments really boils down to two things, loving God and others and treating them accordingly.

We can use this time just before meditation to clean the slate with God by confessing any wrongdoings and purposing to make it right with those we may have offended or hurt. Sometimes that is not possible; yet in any event, we can confess our hurt, pain, and even our anger towards God and receive His love, healing, and forgiveness. By doing so, we remove any dark clouds from our hearts and spirits. Just asking integrates God into the situation, and He will help us to see the situation differently or even change us so we're not so affected by the hurtful ways of others.

Here is a beautiful prayer by Marilyn Morgan Helleberg that I think is a wonderful opening prayer for meditation (I've made some modifications). Over time, your prayers will come naturally. Feel free to add onto this prayer to express what is in your heart to God:

> *Lord Jesus Christ, in this moment and for all eternity, I offer you my body, mind, heart, soul, and spirit, and dedicate to you whatever work you may want to do through me. Help me to be unerringly true to the inner voice - Your Voice.*
>
> *I expect it (You) to surprise me with truths I didn't know I knew- truths that will inspire, uplift, and unify me and those around me. Help me to let go of the ground of rigid rationality for the sake of the creative, intuitively leap that touches the hem of your garment. Help me to erase my little ego-self in the vastness of your message. Let your love and light hover over this meditation practice and may your spirit come to rest, gently and warmly, in my heart, mind, and soul. Amen.*

Journaling- Write it Out:

1. Examine your heart, has there been anything burdening you that you need to confess to God and receive healing?

   _____

   _____

   _____

   _____

2. If so, write out a short prayer, laying this burden on the altar. Even if you aren't ready to let it go, pray that God helps you in this area.

   _____

   _____

   _____

   _____

3. I love the passage, "I could see peace instead of this." What does that say to you?

   _____

   _____

   _____

Prayer of Invitation:

Father God, I invite you into my meditation practice today. So often, I attempt to please you with my own limited understanding, but your ways are not my ways. I want this time with you to be sacred and beneficial. That means you must be in the midst of it. Please reveal to me anything that I need to confess to you. I desire to receive your healing and above all I want to be pleasing to you. I dedicate my meditation practice to you and give you full reign to guide me for your good. Amen.

Day 5:
Let's Meditate

There are many ways to meditate, even as a Christian. Today, you will learn a simple technique that you can use anytime or anywhere, but especially during your quiet time with God. This method is called Sacred Word Meditation.

First, you'll need to select a sacred word or short phrase to meditate on like "Jesus," "Peace be still," "Faith," "God," "Yeshua," "In Him," "Father," or "Love." Whichever word you select, use that same word for the rest of the week.

Your sacred word or phrase, in addition to your breath, helps to keep your mind anchored on God and the present moment during the meditation. If desired, playing soft music in the background can also help ground the mind, but don't make it a crutch for meditation.

During the meditation, whenever your mind begins to wander off, just bring it back to the present moment, back to God, by silently repeating your sacred word or focusing on your breath. Allow your breath to find its natural rhythm. To get started, find a quiet location where you won't be distracted. Next, set a timer for 5, 10, 15, or 20 minutes and then sit in a comfortable position with your back erect.

Close your eyes and then take in 4-5 deep belly breaths to relax. Notice any tension in your body and relax these body parts as well. Now begin to slowly and silently repeat your sacred word or phrase. When your mind wanders off, bring it back to the present by starting to repeat it again. Continue until your timer goes off.

Variations for the meditation: Focus on your breath during the meditation and then only repeat your sacred word/phrase once you've noticed your mind has wandered off, then go back to focusing on your breath.

If you would like to listen to a guided audio version of this meditation to follow, Click here or go to https://thechristianmeditator.com/meditation-audio. I would suggest giving both a try as you are learning this week.

My Meditation Experience. Today's Date: _____.

I meditated for _____ minutes.

Meditating for me today was…

My thoughts during meditation consisted of…

The most difficult part of the meditation was…

During the meditation I felt…

What did I learn about myself today by meditating?

What else did you experience during the meditation?

Anything else worth noting?

Meditation Journaling Sample Answers

Below is a meditation journal sample to show what your entries might look like. This is one I did recently.

- Meditating for me today was… *Peaceful and calming, it took the edge off the anxiety I was feeling.*

- My thoughts during meditation consisted of… *Stuff about an upcoming retreat, adding an additional section to book.*

- The most difficult part of the meditation was… *Doing it! I kind of want to skip it today, but I'm so glad I didn't. It was just what I needed to ground myself in God and Spirit.*

- During the meditation, I felt… *I felt at peace and really happy to be in God's presence.*

- What did I learn about myself today by meditating? *That I need this practice every day if I want to connect with God, myself, and maintain my peace of mind.*

- What else did you experience during the meditation? *Just some wandering thoughts about this and that.*

- How did the meditation experience compare to the one yesterday? *I felt I entered into God's presence much more quickly.*

- Anything else worth noting? *Father, I commit unto you all my cares and worries, and I thank you in advance for guiding me step by step and providing me with everything I need to be whole, successful, and grounded in you alone.*

Day 6:
Observing Your Thoughts

This week is all about learning how to meditate and developing a practice. Instead of giving you a whole morning routine of activities to do, we will concentrate on one and then incorporate others as we move forward. Building a strong meditation foundation, I believe, is essential to developing a deeper and more rewarding relationship with God. As we learn to remove the mental clutter, limiting beliefs, fear-based attitudes by becoming aware of our unconscious thoughts, we make more space for God's spirit to not only speak to us but occupy us as well. So, today we're focusing on our meditation practice to observe our thoughts and the messages they are giving to us.

To get started, find a quiet location where you won't be distracted. Next, set a timer for 5, 10, 15, or 20 minutes and then sit in a comfortable position with your back erect. If you started with 5 minutes yesterday, see if you can extend it to 10 minutes today.

Close your eyes and then take in 4-5 deep belly breaths to relax. Notice any tension in your body and relax these body parts as well. Now begin to slowly and silently repeat your sacred word or phrase.

During the meditation, just notice your thoughts by becoming aware of them. Observe them as a detached bystander. Don't apply any judgment or meaning to them. You can even label each thought that arises with a word that represents its origin like "past," "present," "future," "worry," "fear," "chores," and the like. Allow each thought to dissipate naturally, always coming back to your breath and/or sacred word to ground you in the present moment. Continue until your timer goes off.

Variations for the meditation: Focus on your breath during the meditation and then only repeat your sacred word/phrase once you've noticed your mind has wandered off, then go back to focusing on your breath.

If you would like to listen to a guided audio version of this meditation to follow, **Click here** or go to https://thechristianmeditator.com/meditation-audio . I would suggest giving both a try as you are learning this week.

My Meditation Experience. Today's Date: _____.

I meditated for _____ minutes.

Meditating for me today was…

My thoughts during meditation consisted of…

The most difficult part of the meditation was…

During the meditation, I felt…

What did I learn about myself today by meditating?

What else did you experience during the meditation?

How did the meditation experience compare to the one yesterday?

Anything else worth noting?

Matthew 12:35 "A good man brings good things out of the good stored up in him,"

Day 7:
Am I Meditating Correctly?

If you've been struggling for the last few days with your meditation practice, don't fret. Although conceptually meditation seems easy, it can be quite difficult to do. This is why I believe people need meditation instruction, a meditation support group, or a journal like this one.

Many people do actually meditate incorrectly. I don't mean you. Their whole idea of meditation is to still their bodies, but inside, their minds are driving them bonkers. Some term this "monkey mind" as the mind is jumping from one thought to the next.

After a short while, they say things like, "This meditation stuff doesn't work" and then they give up. The only bad meditation is the one you don't do. It takes time and skill to quiet the mind and detach from its constant yacking. Each time you meditate, even if you can't see it, you are progressing. Therefore, if you are following the steps I have outlined, you're doing it right. Doctors will tell their patients it sometimes takes 6-weeks to see the benefits of some medications, just substitute that word for meditation. Hopefully, you will notice results sooner, but don't give up before you do.

During meditation, you are likely to encounter many distractions. Most of the distractions will be internal, coming from your mind and thoughts; however, external noises may also be prevalent. Do your best to see all noise, whether internal or external as a distraction to pull you away from your practice. Notice outside distractions like car noise, horns, children play, or even the AC and let them pass right through you. Release the need to fight against, become annoyed with, or remove all distractions from your surroundings. These are a part of life. Meditation brings awareness to these distractions allowing us to notice them, but not become overtaken by them.

Today, select and repeat either of the meditation techniques you learned in the previous lessons: Sacred Word or Observing the Breath. To get started, find a quiet location where you won't be distracted. Next, set a timer for 5, 10, 15, or 20 minutes and then sit in a comfortable position with your back erect. If you started with 10 minutes yesterday, see if you can extend it to 15 minutes today.

Close your eyes and then take in 4-5 deep belly breaths to relax. Notice any tension in your body and relax these body parts as well. Now begin to slowly and silently repeat your sacred word or phrase or watch your thoughts.

When your mind wanders off, bring it back to the present by starting to repeat it again. Continue until your timer goes off.

Variations for the meditation: Focus on your breath during the meditation and then only repeat your sacred word/phrase once you've noticed your mind has wandered off, then go back to focusing on your breath.

 If you would like to listen to one of the guided audio versions of these meditations, go to: https://thechristianmeditator.com/meditation-audio . I would suggest giving both a try as you are learning this week.

My Meditation Experience. Today's Date: _____.

I meditated for _____ minutes.

Meditating for me today was…

My thoughts during meditation consisted of…

The most difficult part of the meditation was…

During the meditation, I felt…

What did I learn about myself today by meditating?

What else did you experience during the meditation?

How did the meditation experience compare to the one yesterday?

Psalm 5:3 "In the morning, LORD, you hear my voice; in the morning I lay my requests before you and wait expectantly."

Day 8:
What You Can Feel You Can Heal

Another reason for meditation's transformative effects is its ability to bring up stuff we'd rather bury forever. We all have stuff in our closet that if truth is known, we'd shudder in shame or fear. Just a gentle warning, a regular meditation practice is going to bring your stuff to the surface. Luckily, not all at once as we'd be quite overwhelmed, but as the spirit leads it.

Using meditation as a tool for healing can help you to make peace with your past, your present, and the future. As long as we can be hurt, get upset, or encounter a crisis, we will need inner healing, cleansing, and purging. And as I stated in an earlier section, God puts the onus on us to rid ourselves of all that contaminates body and spirit.

During today's meditation, I want you to focus on the sensations you feel in your body. Because we hold our issues in our tissues, many of us have emotional blocks in our bodies. These blocks are created when we don't release our pain but internalize it instead. Emotional blocks can show up in many different ways, including physical illness or toxic emotions. During the meditation today, if any emotional sensations like fear, anxiety, anger, hurt, insecurity, confusion, sadness, or the like shows up, know that it's revealed itself for a reason. Now, go a little bit deeper to see if you can discover what triggered the sensation. It wants you to acknowledge it, so you can release it and let it go.

How do you let it go? By feeling it as intently as you can. I call this bringing it to the light of God. In God, there is no darkness and His light heals and transforms all who encounter it. As you notice the sensation, invite it to come up. Notice where you feel it most in your body. If you begin to feel afraid or anxious, take in some deep belly breaths. You can even silently repeat your sacred word or phrase. Also, silently ask God to invade the sensation with His healing light. If you want, see God's light penetrating this space in your imagination. Continue to feel and breath until the sensation dissipates.

Please note: In some cases, you may need to seek out a counselor if you discover you just can't handle some of these toxic emotions on your own. You may need someone professional to help you work through some dramatic experiences in your past.

To get started, find a quiet location where you won't be distracted. Next, set a timer for 5, 10, 15, or 20 minutes and then sit in a comfortable position with your back erect. If you started with 15 minutes yesterday, see if you can extend it to 20 minutes today.

Close your eyes and then take in 4-5 deep belly breaths to relax. Notice any tension in your body and relax these body parts as well. Now begin to slowly and silently repeat your sacred word or phrase. When your mind wanders off, bring it back to the present by starting to repeat it again. Become aware of any sensations that arise and go through the procedure above. You can also think about a painful experience as well to invoke uncomfortable emotions for healing. If you don't feel any sensations, that's okay, just focus on your sacred word/phrase and breath. Keep going until your timer goes off.

Variations for the meditation: If no particular sensations are showing up all by themselves, think back to a situation that hurt or angered you. Use the meditation instructions above to release the emotional attachment to it so you can let it go for good.

 If you would like to listen to a guided audio version of this meditation to follow, **Click here** or go to https://thechristianmeditator.com/meditation-audio .

If you are a Listening Library Member or have The Christian Meditation App (when available), I have a guided meditation called, Releasing Toxic Emotions that you can listen to as well. But today, try the one above.

My Meditation Experience. Today's Date: _____.

I meditated for _____ minutes.

Meditating for me today was…

My thoughts during meditation consisted of…

The most difficult part of the meditation was…

During the meditation, I felt the following sensations…

I discovered that I need to heal from …

What else did you experience during the meditation?

How did the meditation experience compare to the one yesterday?

Anything else worth noting?

Psalm 62:5 "For God alone, O my soul, wait in silence, for my hope is from him."

Day 9:
Where is God in All this Meditating?

By now you might be wondering, "Where is God in all of this meditating?" So far, you've meditated to observe your thoughts and feel your feelings, yet, how does all of this make me "closer to God", the real reason you started this journal. Let me answer the question above first, "The Spirit of God is within you." Read the full scripture below:

> *"And when He was demanded of the Pharisees when the kingdom of God should come, He answered them and said, the kingdom of God cometh not with observation: Neither shall they say, lo here! Or, lo there! For, behold, the kingdom of God is within you."* (Luke 17:20-21 King James Version (KJV))

Guess what? You don't have to go to church to find God! You don't even have to go on a spiritual pilgrimage to the Holy Land or some other destination. You don't have to go anywhere but inside of yourself. The church and scriptures may point you to God, but unless you have your own personal experience with God, it's all just words on paper. 2 Corinthians 3:6 says, "… that the Spirit gives life."

John 4:24 also declares, *"God is Spirit, and those who worship Him must worship in spirit and truth."* God doesn't want our works, our service, or our sacrifices unless they are specifically birthed of Him.

But what He wants, even more, is YOU, and that can only come from a purified heart and mind. Even Jesus said, *"These people honor me with their lips, but their heart is far from me."*- (Matthew 15:8)

Spiritual Christians meditate because it helps them to access God already living within them. So many Christians want more than a church relationship, instead, they want a real encounter with God. They want to become one with God just as Jesus said, "I and the Father are one." Meditation takes us to the inward places that God dwells so we can experience His presence. When we decrease our thoughts and ego, we make greater space for God to reside within.

In today's meditation, you're going to acknowledge your oneness with Father God, by silently repeating during the meditation, "My Father and I are one. One body, one mind, one spirit."

As you silently repeat these words, if possible, lose yourself in God's presence. You can use imagery of being engulfed in God's light or feel the warmth of His love. Open your heart fully to receiving Christ within you.

To get started, find a quiet location where you won't be distracted. Next, set a timer for 15 or 20 minutes and then sit in a comfortable position with your back erect. You can play soft music in the background if you desire.

Close your eyes and then take in 4-5 deep belly breaths to relax. Notice any tension in your body and relax these body parts as well.

Now begin to slowly and silently repeat "My Father and I are one. One body, one mind, one spirit." You can say silently, one or more words at a time in alignment with your breath or even the whole thing at once, pausing a few moments in-between. When your mind wanders off, bring it back to the present by starting to repeat it again. Continue until your timer goes off.

Variations for the meditation: Focus on your breath during the meditation and then only repeat your phrase above once you've noticed your mind has wandered off, then go back to focusing on your breath.

My Meditation Experience. Today's Date: _____.

Meditating for me today was…

My thoughts during meditation consisted of…

The most difficult part of the meditation was…

During the meditation, I felt…

What did I learn about myself today by meditating…?

What else did you experience during the meditation?

How did the meditation experience compare to the one yesterday?

Anything else worth noting?

Philippians 4:8 "Finally, brothers and sisters, whatever is true, whatever is noble, whatever is right, whatever is pure, whatever is pure, whatever is lovely, whatever is admirable — if anything is excellent or praiseworthy — think about such things."

Day 10:
Scripture and Passage Meditation

Today I want to introduce you to a new meditation technique called Scripture or Passage Meditation. This technique is pretty much how it sounds. You meditate on a portion of scripture or a favorite spiritual or inspirational passage. This method of meditating on the Lord is to silently repeat a passage of scripture in alignment with your breath.

We become what we meditate on. As we meditate on the scriptures or inspirational passages, these words begin to drop down in our spirit and transform us from within, beginning with our heart. As we continue with the practice, whether it takes days, months, or years, we will be changed.

Through scripture meditation we learn how to quiet our minds and control our thoughts. If you have read any literature or articles on my website, you know that I am continually sharing that the mind is the greatest enemy of the believer. The war against the mind is real but we have the power to renew our minds and make them work for us instead of against us. If you are not consciously controlling your mind, then your mind is controlling you and most of us are completely unaware of it.

"But now I am fearful, lest that even as the serpent beguiled Eve by his cunning, so your minds may be corrupted and seduced from wholehearted and sincere and pure devotion to Christ! "- 2 Cor. 10:4-5; 11:3

Our minds need to be under the control of the Spirit. Corruption of the mind starts at a very young age and unless we're renewing our minds on a regular basis, we can't live our best lives. One of the best ways to check the mind is through the emotions. When we're feeling peaceful, joyful, and content, our minds are projecting the right messages. However, if we're feeling depressed, unhappy, restless, or anxious, our minds are most likely in a revolving pattern of fear and negativity. We can use scripture, passage, or any other of the meditations in this journal to quiet the mind and release our cares to Father God.

Passage and scripture meditation are similar to sacred word meditation, but instead of meditating on just a word or short phrase, you will meditate on an entire scripture, a series of scriptures, or even spiritual passages. If you are familiar with the *Lord's Prayer* or Psalms 23, *The Lord is my Shepherd*, both are great scripture passages to meditate on. Scripture meditation is the ultimate way of hiding God's Word in your heart.

The Lord's Prayer

> *"Our Father who art in heaven, hallowed be thy name. Thy kingdom come. Thy will be done, on earth as it is in heaven. Give us this day our daily bread; and forgive us our trespasses, as we forgive those who trespass against us; and lead us not into temptation, but deliver us from evil."- Matthew 6:9-13*

So, how to do scripture or passage meditation? First, you'll need to select a scripture or passage to meditation on. Again, it can be just one scripture or even a series. If you have memorized a lot of scripture, you can go from one scripture to the next. You don't have to repeat the same one over and over again. Once you have decided on your scripture or passage, follow the steps below:

Begin to repeat your memorized passage as slowly as possible in your mind. There should be about 2-3 seconds between each word. Repeat the passage over and over again until the timer goes off. You can add additional passages you have memorized as well. I sometimes meditate on 4-5 different passages at a time (one after the other).

Whenever your mind wanders off, just bring it back to the scripture passage. You can start at the beginning of the passage, at the beginning of the sentence, or just begin where you left off.

Don't get caught up in your thoughts, whether good, bad, or spiritual, just observe them and return to repeating the scripture passage.

After the meditation, you can spend a few moments in silence, journaling, or reading the Bible or another spiritual book.

(▷) If you would like to listen to a guided audio version of this meditation to follow, Click Here or **go to** https://thechristianmeditator.com/meditation-audio .

My Meditation Experience. Today's Date: _____.

I meditated for _____ minutes.

Meditating for me today was…

My thoughts during meditation consisted of…

The most difficult part of the meditation was…

During the meditation, I felt…

What did I learn about myself today by meditating?

What else did you experience during the meditation?

How did the meditation experience compare to the one yesterday?

Anything else worth noting?

Day 11:
Daily Self-Care Routine

Most people would never consider going days, let alone weeks, neglecting their outer bodies, hygiene, showering, hair, teeth, or changing their clothes. But think about it, most of us have gone years holding onto old resentments, unforgiveness, shame, fear, and more. Jesus told his disciples that it's not what a man puts in his mouth that makes him unclean, but instead what comes out of his heart.

Your daily meditation practice is what helps to cleanse you from the inside out. There are days that I come home from work feeling upset, down, or weary and can't wait to release all of these invisible weights to God through meditation. Using any one of the meditation methods I shared with you this past week, I enter into God's presence and allow Him to cleanse me of any burdens I may be carrying around.

This is why I consider a daily meditation practice an essential part of any self-care routine. When many of us think about self-care, images of full-body massages, pedicures, and healthy eating surface, but self-care must also encompass the spiritual or inner-being. We must be diligent in cleansing our hearts from all the negativity that abounds around us. Charles Stanley hit the nail on the head, when he said in one of his sermons years ago, "It's just going to get on you (negativity)."

When you think about your date with God and meditation practice, please see it as a necessity that will maintain and enhance your overall well-being. Everything starts with the mind. If the mind is out of whack, it impacts every aspect of your life. Research shows that 80-85% of all illness has an emotional root, and that root begins with the mind and the thoughts you are thinking. Healthy mind, healthy life.

Tomorrow we will incorporate a new discipline with our meditation practice. By the end of the journal, you will have a plethora of spiritual practices that you can incorporate into your date with God morning or evening routine. Some will really resonate with you and others you may set aside for later. Being one with God is being led by the spirit and we also need different things at different times in our lives.

Today we're going to continue with our practice of scripture or passage meditation.

You can pick any scripture you have memorized or keep it simple by meditating on "Perfect love casts out fear."- (1 John 4:18) BTW, you don't need to repeat the scripture reference. Your meditation would look something like this on paper, "Perfect (pause) love (pause) casts (pause) out (pause) fear (pause)." Then repeat. I noticed that on the inhale I say each word and then pause on the exhale.

Since you are pretty much a pro now, try this scripture meditation for a full 20 minutes if time permits. To get started, find a quiet location where you won't be distracted. Sit in a comfortable position with your back erect. Close your eyes and then take in 4-5 deep belly breaths to relax. Notice any tension in your body and relax these body parts as well. Now begin to slowly and silently repeat the scripture. When your mind wanders off, bring it back to whichever word you remember stopping at, then repeat from the beginning. You can play soft music in the background if you desire.

If you would like to listen to a guided audio version of this meditation to follow, Click Here or **go to** https://thechristianmeditator.com/meditation-audio .

My Meditation Experience. Today's Date: _____.

I meditated for _____ minutes.

Meditating for me today was…

My thoughts during meditation consisted of…

The most difficult part of the meditation was…

During the meditation, I felt…

What did I learn about myself today by meditating?

What else did you experience during the meditation?

How did the meditation experience compare to the one yesterday?

Anything else worth noting?

Matthew 12:35 "A good man brings good things out of the good stored up in him,"

Day 12:
Checking In & Taking Inventory

Do you ever wake up worried, frustrated, or weighed down? If you don't work on eliminating those toxic emotions, you'll just carry them throughout your day. They will interfere with your joy and peace of mind. They may distract you from what you need to accomplish or drain your energy.

Unfortunately, many people just live with these daily weights and burdens when they can use their date with God to rid themselves of them. Just imagine the accumulated effect of layers and layers of negative thoughts, fear-based thinking, and toxic emotions. It's debilitating. In the previous section, I included some key scriptures regarding purifying our hearts and minds. Re-read them if you need a refresher.

God desires us to purify our minds and cleanse our hearts of everything that will distract us, weigh us down, attack our faith, and hinder our relationship with Him. So, the first step is to take inventory of your mental and emotional state. This will help you to set an intention for your time with God or what you want to accomplish with it.

In addition to observing our thoughts and emotions, I also use this time to get real with God and myself. He knows it all anyway. During my check-in today, I was feeling a little disconnected from God, so I wrote:

> *"Today I feel dissatisfied with my relationship with God. The Bible says to be in the world but not of the world. Lord, please remove the tentacles of the world from my heart and set me free from the addictions of apathy, complacency, and fear. I ask the Holy Spirit to free me from the bondages and illusions of this world and reveal to me areas that need God's healing and light. "*

This is your opportunity to bare all, come clean before the Lord, and boldly approach the throne of grace. Give everything to the Lord and then thank Him for the victory. Even if you feel powerless over the situation, with God nothing is impossible. There have been times I have been very angry with a family member, holding a grudge, and not willing to forgive. During my date with God, I may tell the Lord that I know I need to forgive this person, but I really can't or don't want to. Then I would say something like, "Lord, I need your help. Change my heart. Intervene in this situation." After that, I'd just try to forget about it and go about my business.

I'm always amazed at how God just fixes things without my help or effort. Usually, within a few days, all the anger is gone, and things are back to normal.

It's as if God just reached down into my heart, touched it, and restored my peace and joy. To get started take a few moments to go inside your heart and feel. Then ask yourself the following question, "What am I feeling today?" Once you have connected with your inner being, write your thoughts or feelings in the appropriate section of the Christian Meditation Journal below. At first, you may be surprised at how hard it is to really know what's going on inside you.

We're so used to denying our feelings and putting on a Christian happy face or burying our hurts and disappointments way down within. At other times, we sweep how we feel under the rug, but, reality check here, if you looked under the rug, the dirt is still there. The key to this exercise is not to hide what you feel, but to expose it 100 percent. I call this 'bringing it to the light.' God already knows what's going on, but once you recognize it too, you and God can deal with it together.

I'll have you do the "Checking In" step in the beginning so if you have any issues that are weighing you down or stealing your joy, you can use your meditation practice to release and let them go. Choose any of the Christian meditation methods that you've learned already.

My Meditation Experience. Today's Date _____.

Activity # 1- Checking In
    Today I feel…

Activity # 2 – Meditation: _____ **(method I used)**

    I meditated for _____ minutes.

    Meditating for me today was…

    My thoughts during meditation consisted of…

Meditation helped me to release… Afterwards, I felt…

What can you commit to God today? (Casting your cares on Him)

Any additional inspirations or messages from God to you?

Psalm 5:3 "In the morning, LORD, you hear my voice; in the morning I lay my requests before you and wait expectantly."

Day 13:
Set an Intention

Once you've **Checked In** with yourself, how about creating an intention for your quiet time as well. You can do this by first, asking yourself what you want to get out of today or your time with God? What do you want or need from God right now?

During the **Checking In** and after taking a brief inventory of how you're feeling, perhaps you've honed in on some negative thoughts. You can set an intention to restore your peace of mind or get centered and grounded in Christ. If you're feeling sad or depressed, you may want God to comfort you or to help you let go of toxic emotions. If you have a physical need that you've been worrying about, you can make your intention to ask God for what you need and then to trust and cast all your cares upon Him.

If you're not sure, ask the Holy Spirit to guide you and help you create one. Your intention can help to set the course of your day as well, making both more meaningful and beneficial to you.

I have followed many big influencers over the year and most of them start every day with focus and a plan. Leaving our day to chance leaves us vulnerable to outside forces that pull for our attention and make us less productive. This often leads to being busy with unimportant tasks or temptation; however, when we make a written plan of what we want to accomplish, we're more likely to get it done. Having an intention for our quiet time gives God and ourselves more clarity of what we really need.

Today, in addition to inviting God into your quiet time, write your intention for this time or even for your day as well. For example, "My intention for my quiet time is to release the burdens I feel about my brother," and/or "My intention for today is to be more aware of God's presence."

Today, practice any of the meditations techniques you've learned thus far. If you would like to listen to guided audio versions of these meditations Click Here or **go to** https://thechristianmeditator.com/meditation-audio .

My Meditation Experience. Today's Date _____.

Activity # 1- Checking In. Today I feel…

Activity # 2- My Intention for my date with God is…

Activity # 3 – Meditation: _____ (method I used)

I meditated for _____ minutes.

Meditating for me today was…

My thoughts during meditation consisted of…

Meditation helped me to release… Afterwards, I felt…

What can you commit to God today? (Casting your cares on Him)

Any additional inspirations or messages from God to you?

Day 14:
Closing Prayer

I like to close my date with God by reciting The Lord's Prayer. When the disciples asked Jesus how to pray, this is the prayer he recited, so how can we go wrong. I believe this is the perfect prayer. In addition to the Lord's Prayer, close with any heartfelt words, praises, or gratitude for your time with the Lord.

Our Father, who art in heaven,
Hallowed be thy name.
Thy kingdom come.
Thy will be done, on earth as it is in heaven.
Give us this day our daily bread.
And forgive us our trespasses,
as we forgive those who trespass against us.
And lead us not into temptation,
but deliver us from evil.
For thine is the kingdom, and the power,
and the glory, for ever and ever.
Amen.

My Meditation Experience. Today's Date _____.

Activity # 1- Checking In. Today I feel…

Activity # 2- My Intention for my date with God is…

Activity # 3 – Meditation: _____ (method I used)

I meditated for _____ minutes.

Meditating for me today was…

My thoughts during meditation consisted of…

Meditation helped me to release… Afterwards, I felt…

What can you commit to God today? (Casting your cares on Him)

Any additional inspirations or messages from God to you?

Activity # 4 – Closing Prayer

Today, write out a short closing prayer that you can pray at the conclusion of your meditation time. You can incorporate the Lord's Prayer or any other scriptures that come to mind. Read your closing prayer sealing the deal of your time with God!

beyond
the
basics

Moving Beyond the Basics

So far in the Christian Meditation Journal, we covered what I call the basics. These include Checking In, Setting an Intention, and Christian Meditation, which encompass the three core activities of this program. These can be done successfully in a minimal amount of time. Doing these regularly will help you at minimum, start each day refreshed and renewed, deepen your relationship with God, and start each day with more focus and purpose.

You may be thinking, "Wow," that's a lot of benefit for such a little amount of time. You may even be skeptical that all this can really happen. It can and will if you will be consistent. As you practice these spiritual disciplines regularly, progressively you will begin to see changes in yourself and eventually in your life, without you having to try, strive, or make lots of effort. Every time you enter into God's presence, you are being transformed as God removes layers and layers of conditioning and molds you into His likeness. He is the potter and we are the clay. When we surrender ourselves to God's presence, He performs the work within us. All you need to do is show up.

But the basics are just the basics. For some of you, the basics are just fine for now, and there is NO judgment. If you can stick with only the basics, your life will change for the better for sure; however, many want to go past the basics to something more substantial and grander. That's what we'll be focusing on from this point.

You will still do the three core activities each day, but now I'm going to introduce you to additional spiritual disciplines (The Sides) that you may (or may not) want to incorporate in your morning routine as well. Adding these spiritual disciplines, as needed, will help you grow in various other areas of your life that include: fellowship with God, creating a mission statement for your life, manifesting your dreams, getting physically healthier, learning God's word, organizing your day, and more. The goal isn't for you to do ALL of these things every day, but to pick and choose based upon what you need in this season of your life and the time you have to devote to spiritual self-care.

The goal really is to try it and if you like it, complete the tasks and then incorporate it into your morning routine or keep it on your shortlist for when you need it.

Day 15:
Praise and Worship

There is nothing better than praise and worship to usher in the presence of God. All of us have favorite praise and worship songs that help us to experience God's love and joy. Praise and worship can also be used as a transition from being carnally-minded to spiritually tuned-in. In other words, if some days you just don't "feel" like keeping your appointment with God, use praise and worship music to get you in the mood. It almost never fails. Praise and worship doesn't have to be long. Just one song or two of your favorite worship songs may be all you need to get your mind on the things of God and ready to devote your morning to God.

My favorite Christian music group is Hillsong United. Their songs are anointed and moving. If you like, create a Christian praise and worship mix or find one on YouTube. Once you find one, download it to your computer and burn a CD or add it to your smartphone. You can find websites on the internet that will help you to quickly download YouTube videos and/or convert them into audio files (mp3) for free.

Continue to praise God throughout your date with Him by thanking Him or giving honor to His name. Here are some examples of how David lifted up God in praise and worship:

"I will give thanks to the LORD because of His righteousness; I will sing the praises of the name of the LORD Most High." Psalms 7:17

"The LORD lives! Praise be to my Rock! Exalted be God my Savior!" Psalms 18:46

"Therefore, I will praise you, LORD, among the nations; I will sing the praises of your name." Psalms 18:49

"Great is the LORD, and most worthy of praise…" Psalms 48:41

Today, you will use praise and worship to open up your time with God. Please note, that when you are ready to establish your personal daily routine, you may exclude some of these spiritual disciplines for lack of time or even interest. That's okay. My desire is to introduce these to you so that you have a variety of activities to choose from.

Some days you may spend your whole quiet time doing nothing but praise and worship if you're deeply experiencing God's presence. Praise and worship is just another great way to tune into God and release our burdens. The great thing is that you can make this time your own. I don't believe in one-size-fits-all or cookie-cutter formulas when it comes to fellowshipping with God. We all serve God in our own style and way.

⊳ Here is a link to a few of my favorite praise and worship songs for you to try. **Go to** https://thechristianmeditator.com/meditation-audios

My Meditation Experience. Today's Date _____.

Activity # 1- Praise and Worship - Today I listened to:

Activity # 2- Checking In. Today I feel…

Activity # 3- My Intention for my date with God is…

Activity # 4 – Meditation: _____ (method I used)

I meditated for _____ minutes.

Meditating for me today was…

My thoughts during meditation consisted of…

Meditation helped me to release… Afterwards, I felt…

What can you commit to God today? (Casting your cares on Him)

Any additional inspirations or messages from God to you?

Psalm 19:14 "May these words of my mouth and this meditation of my heart be pleasing in your sight, LORD, my Rock and my Redeemer."

Day 16:
Daily Devotional Reading

Do you have a favorite devotional that keeps your mind centered on Christ or the things of God? For me, that devotional is the *Jesus Calling* by Sarah Young. I have given this devotional to so many friends as gifts and can literally see the transformation taking place. Their conversations become more God-centered as they begin to trust the Creator and rely on His Spirit to guide and direct them. Some of the primary reasons I love the Jesus Calling are that its messages emphasize, 1) spending time in God's presence, 2) seeking God with all your heart, mind and strength, and 3) depending on God alone and bringing ALL your cares and concerns to Him.

Here is a sample excerpt out of Sarah Young's *Jesus Calling*:

"Trust Me enough to spend ample time with Me, pushing back the demands of the day. Refuse to feel guilty about something that is so pleasing to Me, the King of the universe. Because I am omnipotent, I am able to bend time and events in your favor. You will find that you can accomplish more in less time after you have given yourself to Me in rich communion. Also, as you align yourself with My perspective, you can sort out what is important and what is not. Don't fall into the trap of being constantly on the go. Many, many things people do in My Name have no value in My kingdom. To avoid doing meaningless works, stay in continual communication with Me. I will instruct you and teach you in the way you should go, I will counsel you with My eye upon you."

When we need to be inspired or even a quick word from God in written form, a daily devotional can really fit the bill. I'm always surprised at how "on-point" the message is for me that day. It's just like God knew what I needed to hear.

In addition, be on the lookout for my new The Christian meditation app that includes daily Christian meditations, tools, and prompts to help you to draw closer to God and experience His presence. Please check the webpage, https://thechristianmeditator.com to see when and if it's available. I'm hoping to have it completed by the end of 2020.

There are different ways to read your devotional. Devotionals like the Daily Bread or Jesus Calling are organized in daily bite-sized messages by days and months; however, I have some devotional guides that are just a compilation of passages like the book, *How God Spoke to Me*. With these, I may just flip to a page and read the passage, asking God to direct me to the message I need for that day.

In addition, I have many spiritual books as well that I may spend a few minutes reading in order or flip to a page (generally after reading it all the way through) to remind me of the many ways of staying on the spiritual path.

A daily devotional can be read in just a few minutes but can have an impact on your whole day by moving your heart from fear to faith, lack to abundance, or doubt to trust.

Again, you can use ANY devotional, but if at all possible, I encourage you to try the *Jesus Calling*. You will not be disappointed. You can even get *Jesus Calling* as a mobile application.

Other Popular Devotionals Include:

Daily Christian Meditations by Rhonda Jones (on YouTube)

Your Needs Met by Jack and Cornella Addington

Daily Word

Daily Bread

The Love Dare

The Utmost for His Highest

A Year with God: Living Out the Spiritual Disciplines

Once you read through the passage, if you desire, write down the central theme of the passage (below). Here, you are summarizing what you read in your own words or what God is saying to you through the narrative. This can be one word, a sentence, or even a paragraph or two. This will help you to internalize the message and take ownership of it for your life. You can even use "I" messages to embed yourself in the text. Once you have recorded your summary in your journal, read it over several times if time permits.

If you don't have a devotional handy, just select and read a short and random passage from one of your favorite spiritual books for 1-3 minutes. I like to find and read passages I've heavily highlighted beforehand.

My Meditation Experience. Today's Date _____.

Activity # 1- Checking In - Today I feel…

Activity # 2- My Intention for my date with God is…

Activity # 3– Meditation

I meditated for _____ minutes.

Meditating for me today was…

My thoughts during meditation consisted of…

Meditation helped me to release …

After the meditation, I felt…

Any additional inspirations or messages from God to you?

Activity # 4- Daily Devotional Reading - Summarize message or inspiration I received today…

Day 17:
Meditate on God's Word

As believers, we are to hide God's Word in our hearts. In fact, the Bible says that those who meditate on the Word of God will have greater success in life. (Joshua 1:8)

God's Word sets a standard for our lives, so it is important that we know what it says. Meditating on God's Word is different than just reading a chapter or passage of scriptures, then putting your Bible away. Reading through the scriptures quickly may only be 'skin deep.' Many people have a hard time understanding some passages or quickly forget what they just read. If you are reading material that has no relevance to your life right now, it's difficult to absorb it. Meditating on the scriptures assures that some portion of scriptures will penetrate your heart, without feeling the pressure to get in your reading quota for the day.

When meditating on God's Word, you read until something in God's Word pricks your heart or jumps off the page like a neon light. It could be one word or an entire verse of scripture. Hebrews 4:12 says that God's Word is like a two-edged sword; it is alive, and it quickens us. We are changed by the Word, but the Word has to get into our hearts and our spirits and not just our minds.

Meditating on the Word, by taking small bites and then chewing on them slowly, is transformative and much more effective than just reading whole chapters or passages.

To practice meditating on God's Word, you will need to start reading a chapter or passage of scripture. These can be random or a part of a Bible reading plan. At the bottom of each page of the *Jesus Calling,* and many other devotionals, are scripture references. You can select one of these for your meditating focus each day. Once selected, start reading the passage until something in the scriptures jumps out at you and appears to have some relevance to your life. Continue to read the rest of the chapter or passages to see if any other portion of scripture relates or stands out.

After reading the passage or chapter, find the specific scriptures that were meaningful to you and highlight them in your Bible. Reread them several times and then write down the most relevant words or passages in your journal.

Once you have written them down, also write how the passage(s) spoke to you. Again, use "I" messages to write in the first person. If time permits, re-read what you wrote one or more times.

You can find Bible reading plans on the internet that will guide you in reading the entire Bible or New Testament in a year. Another option is to pick a book of the Bible and read a chapter per day. Below are the links to several websites that provide Bible Reading Plans. Bible Gateway will actually send you the scripture passage via email each day. There are also daily Bible Apps you can download for free to your smartphone. Some of these will read the passage aloud for you.

http://www.keepandshare.com/doc4/78/reading-plan-new-testament-in-one-year

http://www.scefc.org/documents/52_wks_new_testament.pdf

http://www.biblegateway.com/reading-plans

By meditating on God's Word, you may become interested in exploring additional topics through Bible study at a later time; however, meditating on God's Word is more about getting a Word from God for you today. You can keep this Word close to your heart and meditate on it as your anchor when you need to be strengthened or draw closer to God. Just silently repeating the word "trust" as you are working can keep you grounded in Christ and the Spirit, especially when you're feeling overwhelmed or stressed. This is why I like to narrow the chapter or passage to just a few words or two that I can grasp onto for the day.

Also, when it comes to reading the Bible, I don't understand everything I read (especially in the Old Testament) and sometimes this can cause confusion. Try not to get too hung up on those passages that don't make sense right now. Ask God for discernment and then let them go. Jesus said, "Whatsoever things are true, lovely, and of a good rapport, think on those things." Therefore, I enjoy meditating on the scriptures that build up my spirit as opposed to creating confusion.

My Meditation Experience. Today's Date _____.

Activity # 1- Checking In - Today I feel…

Activity # 2- My Intention for my date with God is...

Activity # 3- Meditation

I meditated for _____ minutes.

Meditating for me today was...

My thoughts during meditation consisted of...

Meditation helped me to release ...

After the meditation, I felt...

Any additional inspirations or messages from God to you?

Activity # 4- Meditating on God's Word

A word, phrase, or passage that stood out for me today...

2 Timothy 2:15 "Study to shew thyself approved unto God, a workman that needeth not to be ashamed, rightly dividing the word of truth."

Day 18:
Prayer & Intercession

Prayer is making your request be made known unto God. If you feel as though God is not doing much in your life these days, perhaps you are not giving Him much to work with. Matthew 21:22 tells us to ask and believe in order to receive. I believe God is activated by our prayers integrated with faith. James 4:2 declares, "Yet you don't have what you want because you don't ask God for it." God gets delighted in answering our prayers according to His will. When we ask and He answers, He gets the glory.

Several years ago, my daughter was abruptly laid off because someone in her office lied on her and basically threw her under the bus to save their own skin. She was devastated because she knew she was doing an exceptional job, and this came out of the left field. I shared with her the three times I had been laid off and how within weeks, I had new jobs that I wasn't even expecting.

The first time I was laid off, I received a call about a job I had applied for a year earlier. The second time, I got a tip about a job from a woman who attended my yard sale and was immediately hired, and the third time, I was hired as an intern teacher at a year-around school, where I could do my student teaching and saved over $7000 in school fees. There was also a fourth time that I was hired after receiving a call from my old employer suggesting that I interview for a brand-new position, which I got.

I let my daughter know that God must have something better for her right around the corner. Over the week I continued to pray and thank the Lord for her new job. I also prayed that God would encourage and comfort my daughter. I was surprised when the next day she seemed happy and motivated. Well, not even a single week went by before she was offered a new job that she had interviewed for, before accepting the previous position. She said that this was the job she had really wanted anyway.

I told her God had to remove her from the old job so she would be available when they called her for the new one! Would this have happened without prayer? It could have, but because I openly prayed, my daughter is thanking God for the victory, and so am I. Use your time with God to put something on God's To-Do List and then give Him the glory when He comes through.

You can also spend your prayer-time just talking to Jesus. Tell Him how you feel and what you need or pray for the needs of others. Once you have completed the guided meditation, you will most likely feel a deeper connection to God and His Spirit. Pray to God verbally, if that feels comfortable. Know that God hears you and is listening (2 Kings 20:5b). Some of my greatest breakthroughs have come from just talking to God like I would a very close friend. You can end this step by thanking God for meeting your needs (by faith, if necessary) and turning any cares over to Him.

Another important aspect of our prayer time is the pardoning of sins. James 5:16 declares, *"Therefore confess your sins to each other and pray for each other so that you may be healed."* 1 John 1: 9 states, *"If we confess our sins, He is faithful and just and will forgive us our sins and purify us from all unrighteousness."* When we confess our wrongdoings to God and ask for forgiveness, we allow God's healing to take place in our lives. When we refuse to repent or harbor unforgiveness, we erode our spirit. We don't hurt others; we're hurting ourselves by allowing that poison to fester in our hearts. You can use your time with God to examine your heart regarding anything that might be hindering the flow of His Spirit in your life. God wants to set us free. Your time with God is a time of cleansing and renewal. If you're not sure you have sinned against God in some way, ask Him to reveal this to you? Ask Him to convict your heart of any wrong-doing, and then listen closely. I believe God will reveal to you any areas you need to bring under His authority or that you need repentance.

I believe that many Christians' hearts have waxed cold. We have allowed compromise, busyness, disobedience, and apathy to suppress the voice of God in our hearts. If we continue to grieve the Holy Spirit by not following His voice or promptings, we will lose this sensitivity to God and what He might be trying to say to us. If you feel like this is you, ask God to soften your heart and restore your ability to hear, experience, and discern the leading of the Holy Spirit. From there, anytime you sense God's voice, yearnings, or presence, listen and obey. I believe the more we surrender to God's presence and guidance, the greater His manifestations will be in our lives. God does not live in darkness; therefore, we must rid ourselves of the mental and spiritual dirt that blocks God's movement and contaminates our hearts. If we want God's full rein living and ruling in us, then we must be a vessel He can use. Use this time of prayer to release and let go of anything that might be standing in the way.

If you are struggling with a particular sin, ask God to deliver you and continue to thank God daily by faith, for the victory and your freedom. Don't allow satan to bring condemnation and make you feel unworthy. The Bible says that *"while we yet sinners, Christ died for us."* God doesn't want you to fight the enemy in your own strength. If you could, He didn't need to come. The Bible says, *"Greater is He that is in you than He who is in the world."* The key to this verse is He that is the "in you." Your victory is in allowing the Holy Spirit, God's Spirit, to abide in you completely. It is the spirit that does the work. Isn't that good news? Zechariah 4:6 says, *"This is the word of the LORD...: 'Not by might nor by power, but by my Spirit,' says the LORD Almighty."* Therefore, instead of trying to fight the sin, just open your mind, body, and heart to more and more of God's Spirit living on the inside of you. Let him saturate you through and through. The more you are filled with God's light, the less of the enemy's darkness can enter in. Repent and seek God's forgiveness for yourself and also forgive others. Don't allow anything to taint your heart and hinder God's love, light, and power from flowing through you. Forgive because you have been forgiven.

In addition, you can list your prayer requests and petitions in a notebook or journal. Again, these can be prayer requests for yourself or others, nations, forgiveness, healing, authority figures, etc. Once you have listed your prayer requests, it is time to pray. I want to encourage you to pray both in the spirit and with understanding. The scripture references below give more details regarding how we are to pray:

> *Philippians 4:6 – "Do not be anxious about anything, but in every situation, by prayer and petition, with thanksgiving, present your requests to God. And the peace of God, which transcends all understanding, will guard your hearts and your minds in Christ Jesus."*

> *Mark 11:24 – "Therefore I tell you, whatever you ask for in prayer, believe that you have received it, and it will be yours."*

> *1 Peter 5:7 – "Cast all your anxiety on Him because he cares for you."*

> *1 Corinthians 14:15 –"So what shall I do? I will pray with my spirit, but I will also pray with my understanding; I will sing with my spirit, but I will also sing with my understanding."*

Romans 8:26- 27 -"In the same way the Spirit also helps our weakness; for we do not know how to pray as we should, but the Spirit Himself intercedes for us with groanings too deep for words; and He who searches the hearts knows what the mind of the Spirit is, because He intercedes for the saints according to the will of God."

Hebrews 4:16- "Let us then approach God's throne of grace with confidence, so that we may receive mercy and find grace to help us in our time of need."

Hebrews 4:12- "For the word of God is alive and active. Sharper than any double-edged sword, it penetrates even to dividing soul and spirit, joints and marrow; it judges the thoughts and attitudes of the heart."

Isaiah 51:55- "so is my word that goes out from my mouth: It will not return to me empty but will accomplish what I desire and achieve the purpose for which I sent it."

Philippians 2:10 –"that at the name of Jesus every knee should bow, in heaven and on earth and under the earth."

Matthew 18:18- "Truly I tell you, whatever you bind on earth will be bound in heaven, and whatever you loose on earth will be loosed in heaven."

First of all, we are to come boldly to the throne of grace. I talk a lot about sheepish prayers in my articles and videos. Sheepish prayers are begging God to move in our lives. I realize that at times the only prayers we can muster up are desperate prayers asking for God's help and strength; however, the majority of our prayer should be with confidence, boldness, and speaking His Word. As we can see from the scriptures above, God's word cannot return void. His word is also alive and active. When we speak God's Word over our situations and/or loved ones, that word goes out to accomplish God's will. Therefore, pray with faith, authority, and expectancy in the Name of Jesus! We are told that the Name of Jesus is above every name and power and that whatever we bind on earth is bound in heaven. In other words, Jesus gave YOU power in His NAME!

Secondly, take all your cares and concerns to the Lord in prayer. That is exactly what *The Christian Meditation Journal* is designed to do. It gives you the opportunity to unload all your worries, fears, and other heavyweights unto the Lord. God doesn't want us to carry these around or even try to figure them out. He wants us to turn them over to Him and then trust Him to work all things out according to His Highest Good for us! That doesn't mean that God won't prompt you to intervene or take action, but when you do, you will be doing so from a place of faith and not fear, from peace and not desperation. By being still and quieting your mind, you also give God the opportunity to speak to you through His still, small voice. Often times, the perfect solution will just pop in your mind unexpectedly when you turn it over and rest in Him.

Lastly, God wants us to pray in the spirit as well as pray with our understanding; praying in the spirit means praying in tongues. You may belong to a denomination that believes God has done away with tongues, but I don't believe that is what the scriptures tell us. For more information about speaking in tongues, read Romans Chapter 8. So why pray in the spirit? I don't know about you, but there are many times that I just don't know what to pray. There may be a burden on my heart, but I'm not sure of the need or even the recipient.

According to Romans 8: 26-27, *"the Spirit Himself intercedes for us with groanings too deep for words… because He intercedes for the saints according to the will of God."* Praying in the spirit allows the Holy Spirit to pray according to the will of God. As stated above, Paul said in 1 Corinthians 14:15, *"I will pray with my spirit, but I will also pray with my understanding."* When we pray in the Spirit we are praying to God, for God is the only one who understands what we are saying. We are praying our heavenly language and not even the devil knows what we are saying. Praying in tongues or the spirit is praying beyond the limitations of our mind.

If you have not received the baptism of the Holy Spirit with the evidence of speaking in tongues, first, ask God to give you this gift. Luke 11: 13 declares, *"How much more will your Father in heaven give the Holy Spirit to those who ask Him!"* Also, read Acts 2: "When the day of Pentecost came, they were all together in one place. Suddenly a sound like the blowing of a violent wind came from heaven and filled the whole house where they were sitting. They saw what seemed to be tongues of fire that separated and came to rest on each of them. All of them were filled with the Holy Spirit and began to speak in other tongues as the Spirit enabled them."

In addition to the above, do some research on this topic. There are many great articles and YouTube videos on receiving the Holy Spirit. Being filled with God's Spirit will add more power and boldness to your Christian walk.

My Meditation Experience. Today's Date: _____.

Activity # 1- Checking In - Today I feel…

Activity # 2- My Intention for my date with God is…

Activity # 3– Meditation

I meditated for _____ minutes.

Meditating for me today was…

My thoughts during meditation consisted of…

Meditation helped me to release …

After the meditation, I felt…

Any additional inspirations or messages from God to you?

Activity # 4- Prayer

Today I pray in faith....

John 1:2 "My dear friend, I pray that everything may go well with you and that you may be in good health—as I know you are well in spirit.""

Day 19:
Express Gratitude

Everything in your life might be falling apart, but there is always something for which to be thankful or grateful. It is surprising to me, just how much impact this little exercise can have. When we begin to think about the good things in our lives, we can have a major attitude shift. If we're honest, the good always outweighs the bad. We just need to be reminded. Expressing gratitude on a daily basis is a self-fulfilling prophecy because the more we appreciate what we have, the more we attract even more things for which to be grateful. Not only that, it's been scientifically proven that those who practice gratitude regularly experience more joy, have a greater sense of well-being, get sick less frequently, have greater family connections, are more optimistic, have more resilience, and are more apt to accomplish their goals.

So, what are you thankful for? You might be grateful for warm feet, a good night's sleep, or an unexpected blessing. It's really the simple things in life that bring us the most joy and happiness. To get you started, think about what brought you joy today, the many blessings in your life, what inspired you, or what brought you peace and comfort.

You can also use gratefulness as a way to script your attitude, day, or future. Here is an easy process. Using the sentence starter, "I'm thankful and grateful..." list all your goals, dreams, and desires as though they already happened. For example, I am thankful and grateful that I'm going to Paris is summer, I have my dream job, or my business is prospering. Be sure to include lots of feelings and emotions. For example, I am feeling so enthusiast because I'm going to have an awesome day. Or, my new job brings me so much joy and contentment. Lastly, reinforce your grateful heart with scripture passages or principles. For example, I am so grateful to God for loving me, meeting my needs, and guiding me every step of the way. You can be general or really specific. Make gratitude writing an ongoing practice. Sometimes I'll write three full pages of things I'm grateful for.

My Meditation Experience. Today's Date _____.

Activity # 1- Checking In - Today I feel…

Activity # 2- My Intention for my date with God is…

Activity # 3– Meditation

I meditated for _____ minutes.

Meditating for me today was…

My thoughts during meditation consisted of…

Meditation helped me to release …

After the meditation, I felt…

Any additional inspirations or messages from God to you?

Activity # 4- Being Grateful

Today I am thankful and grateful for… (list 3 or more things). Or write a full-page gratitude story to script your goals, day, feelings, and God's sovereignty in your affairs.

Thessalonians 5:18 "In
every thing give thanks:
for this is the will of
God in Christ Jesus
concerning you."

Day 20:
Movement or Exercise

It may seem a little awkward that I have included exercise in your time with God, but we're only as good as we feel, and exercise can play a huge role in our mental and emotional well-being. We know from research that regular exercise can be more effective in fighting depression than prescription drugs. Also, when we exercise, especially in the morning, we feel more energized and usually get more done. It can also help to enhance our quiet time and set a great momentum for the day.

You don't have to do anything elaborate or join the gym. Even a short walk, 10 minutes of yoga, or a few choice exercises will do. I have added links to several 10-minute workouts on YouTube. You can find links to these on the private meditation page. Sometimes, I will add a short workout to the beginning and end of my quiet time. Besides walking, I enjoy doing a short morning yoga workout to further establish my inner peace. It's also a great way to get some stretching and strength-building exercises in my routine as well. Remember, a little can go a long way with consistency. After completing the basics, do the yoga sequence, take a short brisk walk, or find a 10-minute (or longer) workout video on YouTube. When completed, you'll really feel as though you've accomplished something. On the meditation-audio page, I have created a link to my *Christian Yoga Challenge* as well.

My Meditation Experience. Today's Date _____.

Activity # 1- Checking In - Today I feel…

Activity # 2- My Intention for my date with God is…

Activity # 3– Meditation

I meditated for _____ minutes.

Meditating for me today was…

My thoughts during meditation consisted of…

Meditation helped me to release …

After the meditation, I felt…

What can you commit to God today?

Any additional inspirations or messages from God to you?

Activity # 4- Move or Exercise

Today my movement or exercise routine will consist of… (i.e. 10 minutes of yoga)

Day 21:
Inspired Reading

Many people have a hard time finding time to read anymore nowadays. It's as though reading has become a lost art. Another way to enhance your time with God is by reading inspirational, self-development, or professional books that will teach you something new or nourish your soul.

Try to make it a habit to read 1-10 pages or one chapter of some book each day. That is what I try to do. Just think, in 30 days, if you read only 10 pages, that's 300 pages and the length of at least one book per month. This is a great way to get your reading in and expand your mind and knowledge.

After reading, in your journal jot down any notes regarding the main idea or any key points that resonated with you. For today, just pick up a book on the shelf that you have eyeing for some time. Books on spirituality, marriage, self-help, health, and nutrition are some good topics.

My Meditation Experience. Today's Date _____.

Activity # 1- Checking In - Today I feel...

Activity # 2- My Intention for my date with God is...

Activity # 3– Meditation

I meditated for _____ minutes.

Meditating for me today was...

My thoughts during meditation consisted of...

Meditation helped me to release ...

After the meditation, I felt...

Any additional inspirations or messages from God to you?

Activity # 4- Inspired Reading- The main idea or key points I learned today that I can apply to my life...

Day 22:
Topical Bible Study

Study to show yourself approved, rightly dividing the word of truth. – 2 Timothy 2:15

Faith comes by hearing and hearing the word of God. - Romans 10:17

If you want to grow in God's Word, you will have to study the scriptures. The Word of God is the foundation of our faith. Without the Word planted deep within our hearts, we can easily be discouraged or led astray. In addition, we need to use the word of God to come against the lies of the enemies. When we are bombarded with thoughts of fear, doubt, and worry, the best thing we can do is use God's word to combat them. In Ephesians 6:16-18, we are to put on the whole armor of God.

> *"In addition to all this, take up the shield of faith, with which you can extinguish all the flaming arrows of the evil one. ¹⁷ Take the helmet of salvation and the sword of the Spirit, which is the word of God. And pray in the Spirit on all occasions with all kinds of prayers and requests. With this in mind, be alert and always keep on praying for all the Lord's people."*

If we don't personally know and use God's word to extinguish the flaming-darts that show up from day to day, we can be constantly defeated in our Christian walk. Having the tools isn't enough, we must use them by putting them into practice.

Even Jesus, when spending 40 days and nights in the wilderness (meditating I presume) used God's word against satan who came to entice Him. Jesus said, *"It is written..."*

If you are struggling in a particular area, like faith, for example, reading Biblical stories of faith, memorizing scriptures of faith, and reading passages on faith can work together to strengthen you in this area. We have too much knowledge available to us to allow ourselves to become victims of our thoughts and circumstances.

I know some Christians who have accepted the Lord, but who have never grown past that first act of salvation because they rarely study the Word. These same Christians rely on the pastor or minister to feed them weekly. I'm sure you'll agree that they are spiritually starving!

These same believers are often characterized as what the Bible says in Ephesians 4:14, "Tossed and blown about by every wind of new teaching," because their walk is not based in sound truth. Therefore, every chance we get, we want to be studying God's Word, and topical Bible Studies are a great way to learn about God's Word in context to a theme or topic of interest.

You can find many of these on the internet or by purchasing a Bible study book. Today, spend 10 minutes studying some aspect of God's Word. To make it easy for today, I have included several links to a specific topic: *Living by Faith.* I literally googled this and found many to choose from. You can add, ".pdf" to the search and get downloadable lessons. Here are two to choose from:

Faith: A Study of Hebrews 11

http://dsntl8idqsx2o.cloudfront.net/wp-content/uploads/sites/4/2013/09/livingbyfaith-dabbs.pdf

How to Live by Faith

http://www.bankspresbyterianchurch.org/wp-content/uploads/2016/08/How-to-Live-by-Faith.pdf

After reading a section for 5-10 minutes or so, you can also look up the scriptures and read them in context and even write any key points or inspiration in your journal. Studying God's Word doesn't have to be a jam session or take hours; in fact, learning in small bites and then applying what you learned is better for retention and growth than reading a whole chapter.

God wants us to be more than hearers of the Word. In your journal, list a few ways you can live out what you've discovered in practical daily terms. For example, "I'm going to have faith in God to meet a particular need." When doubt arises, have scriptures ready to stop the flow of doubtful thoughts; for example, "Stop! My God shall meet all my needs according to His divine riches and glory," with "I trust God beyond what I can see."

My Meditation Experience. Today's Date _____.

Activity # 1- Checking In - Today I feel...

Activity # 2- My Intention for my date with God is...

Activity # 3– Meditation

I meditated for _____ minutes.

Meditating for me today was...

My thoughts during meditation consisted of...

Meditation helped me to release ...

After the meditation, I felt...

Any additional inspirations or messages from God to you?

Activity # 4- Topical Bible Study on Faith

Key points from Bible Study… How can I apply what I learned today…What scripture will I use to combat doubtful thoughts?

Day 23:
Daily Declarations and Affirmations (Part 1)

What you focus on grows. In upcoming lessons, we will focus on theme-based affirmations and daily declarations to attract what we "really" want in our lives.

Did you know that we live the majority of our lives based upon the programming in the subconscious mind? In fact, according to psychologists, we only use 5% of our conscious thinking. Most of what we do is by default. Throughout the better part of our day, we are living on autopilot based upon our belief systems and habits that we're primarily formed before the age of 8-years-old.

Many Christians would say they are NOT living the life of their dreams, but really, they are. That's because what we think about most of the time is what manifests in our lives. Our past, present, current situation and lifestyle are directly related to the thoughts we think and what we believe, and for each person this is different.

Even Jesus said that men manifest from the treasures in his or her heart (Matthew 12:35) and to guard your heart for from the heart comes the issues of life (Proverbs 4:23). If you're not satisfied with your life or are far from living the life of your dreams, you must make changes in your thoughts and belief systems; however, because these beliefs and habits are so deeply rooted into our subconscious mind, it's more than a matter of sheer will-power. With 95% of the subconscious mind running the show, without the right strategies, it's almost a losing battle. Our subconscious mind is like a thermostat set on a specific degree of comfort. We may try to set it to a different temperature, yet without consistent monitoring, it's going to go back to what it knows best.

There are several methods we can use to alter our subconscious minds and make lasting changes, but first, you need to know that the subconscious mind is not your logical mind. Instead, its beliefs are formed either by being in an alpha state (barely-awake) or through repetition, doing something over and over again so that it becomes an unconscious habit, like driving home every day. It also responds to images and visuals.

Some of the best ways to reprogram the subconscious mind are through affirmations and visualization. I will discuss visualization in an upcoming lesson, but today I will address affirmations. First, what are affirmations? Basically, they are intentional statements, said in the affirmative, of what you want. In reality, we are unconsciously saying or thinking affirmations all day long.

Unfortunately, most of these are negative or what we really don't want. Our subconscious doesn't discriminate but gives us what we think about most of the time. You only have to look at your life to see the "dream life" you've created. Not liking what you see, use The Christian Meditation Journal to make changes to your thoughts and beliefs for a new life and outcomes.

Since it takes repetition to reprogram your subconscious mind, you'll need to repeat affirmations or daily declarations over and over. The best times to read your affirmations or daily declarations are at bedtime before you doze off, when you first wake up, right after meditation, or between 1-7 years old (too late for that). These are the times when your subconscious mind is most receptive because you are in a semi-hypnosis state and all its guards are down.

One of the benefits that meditation provides is bringing awareness to our thoughts and emotions. Our emotions tell us whether our thoughts are negative or positive. In addition to the times suggested, use body awareness through-out the day to catch your negative and doubtful thoughts and then replace them with your affirmations. This will help you begin to root out your limiting beliefs and plant new thoughts that you want to grow. See negative thoughts as weeds in your mental garden and pull them up as soon as you notice them; otherwise, you'll just go back to your old mental thermostat.

Another activity I do sometimes is to walk around my house for several minutes declaring my affirmations out loud. I'll start off with, "This is the day the Lord has made, I will rejoice and be glad in it." After that, with enthusiasm, I will declare God's blessings over my life as well as what I want to come to pass. I might say, "I'm so thankful for my best-selling books, my excellent health, and that I am allergy-free." I will also declare God's promises like, "Thank you God for causing all things to work out together for my highest good," and "I am one with God, mind, body, and spirit." Doing this exercise really pumps me up for the day.

Some mornings, before even getting out of bed, I'll turn on affirmations and listen for 5-10 minutes. I'll play my own affirmations (I have many to choose from at https://thechristianmeditator.com), or I'll select a favorite from YouTube. Starting your day and thoughts in a positive way will go a long way in creating internal joy and happiness.

Today, after meditation, make a list of affirmative statements that you want to attract into your life. Jesus said, whatever you ask for if you believe you will receive it, it will be yours. There is a big difference between just saying what you want and believing you'll get it.

Most of us won't right away, but with consistency, we can alter our beliefs. Write at least 10 affirmations. Here are a few examples: I am at my ideal weight; my business is prospering; I have a great marriage; I love my life; I have great friendships; I am living in my dream home; I am in perfect health; my relationship with God continues to grow; and I am living in alignment with my purpose.

My Meditation Experience. Today's Date _____.

Activity # 1- Checking In - Today I feel...

Activity # 2- My Intention for my date with God is...

Activity # 3– Meditation

I meditated for _____ minutes.

Meditating for me today was...

My thoughts during meditation consisted of...

Meditation helped me to release …

After the meditation, I felt…

Any additional inspirations or messages from God to you?

Activity # 4- Affirmations

Write down at least 10 affirmations or positive statements that you want to reprogram into your subconscious mind and then read them aloud. Write them in the affirmative. For example, "I have a healthy and balanced appetite" instead of "I want to stop overeating."

Day 24:
Daily Declarations and Affirmations (Part 2)

Yesterday, you wrote your 10 affirmations. Hopefully throughout the day you caught your negative or fear-based thoughts and replaced them with one of your affirmations instead. When I started doing this many years ago, I noticed that my negative thoughts came so fast I was constantly shooting them down. Over time, my mind quieted down and my depression went away. Every time we have a negative or fear-based thought, we attract other like-thoughts to us. This turns into a spiral of negativity that if not dealt with can turn into a stronghold in our lives in the form of depression, anxiety, or constant worry. Jesus said that it is the "little foxes that destroy the vine," so it's best to deal with them when they first come up and not let them play out a whole drama in our heads.

Something I started doing recently is waking up every morning saying what I am blessed and grateful for. It is generally the first thoughts of the day that set the tone for your thinking and how you're going to feel. Before I even open my eyes, silently I say things like, I'm so grateful for this new day; I'm thankful for a good night sleep; I'm thankful for my family; I'm grateful that my body is healed; I'm grateful that my prospering business"… I may also do this when I go to sleep at night. I can honestly tell you that I wake up most mornings with joy and enthusiasm for my day. If you didn't notice, these are also affirmations and another way to use them.

Next, I want to share with you about daily declarations. Several years ago, I attended a church where each Sunday we'd read daily declarations aloud as a congregation. They were always on different topics and mostly based upon the scriptures. Like God, our words are powerful, they have life, and they cannot return void. Jesus said, "You will have what you say." So why not say and plant words of love, success, faith, power, and peace.

Below is a daily declaration regarding Guidance & Direction. In the appendix, you can find more daily declarations on Loving Yourself, Sound Mind, Abundance & Success, and Health & Wellness. For today, you'll read this one, but your assignment will be to make one of your own that you can read every day when you wake up and before you go to bed. With consistency, your subconscious will pick up on your new programming and begin to work for the things you truly desire.

Daily Declaration for Guidance & Direction

I declare that I am led and guided by the Holy Spirit. I seek first the kingdom of God and everything I need is added unto me. I trust God with all my heart and lean not to my own understanding.

In all my ways I acknowledge Him, and He directs my steps. Because God is for me, He's more than the whole world against me. I wait upon the Lord. God will never leave me or forsake me. I can say with confidence; the Lord is my helper, I will not fear what man can do to me. I am one with God, mind, body, and spirit. My steps are ordered by the Lord. This is my declaration. Amen! (FYI- There are additional pre-written declarations in the appendix.)

My Meditation Experience. Today's Date _____.

Activity # 1- Checking In - Today I feel…

Activity # 2- My Intention for my date with God is…

Activity # 3– Meditation

I meditated for _____ minutes.

Meditating for me today was…

My thoughts during meditation consisted of…

Meditation helped me to release …

After the meditation, I felt…

Any additional inspirations or messages from God to you.

Activity # 4- Daily Declaration

Read the daily declaration above again. Take a few minutes to write your own. Read it before bed tonight and when you first wake up in the morning.

Psalm 19:14 "May these words of my mouth and this meditation of my heart be pleasing in your sight, LORD, my Rock and my Redeemer."

Day 25:
Visualization

Visualization is a powerful spiritual discipline to attract what you want in your life. In studies, athletes who physically practiced a sport or just "imagined" practicing a sport, both improved their game at about the same level. Your imagination is a powerful tool for creation.

And just think about it, everything that exists started with a thought, a visual image, words, and then taking action. Even God had to have a picture in mind when we created the world and we're told in scripture that it's His Word that keeps the universe afloat.

> *"He is the radiance of the glory of God and the exact imprint of His nature, and He upholds the universe by the word of His power…"- Hebrews 1:3*

"Write your vision on the wall and make it plain," says Habakkuk 2:2. Those who know what they want, write it down and visualize it, manifest it much more quickly than those who don't. By visualization, I mean they see it, feel it, touch it, (mentally) and experience it as though it's already happened. Scientists have discovered that our brains don't know the difference between what is real and what is imagined. Just think about eating your favorite food right now and notice the sensations of your mouth and body. You're experiencing it in your subconscious mind. This is one reason that vision boards are so popular. Not only do you get clear on your vision, you find images that also represent it.

About 4 years ago, I had a knee injury. I had a few natural treatments done that alleviated the pain. That was until I started to play racket ball and problems in my knee began to resurface. This included pain when walking that started to become somewhat debilitating. So, after starting physical therapy again, I decided that I would do two additional things 1) Go on a cleansing fast to eliminate toxins that might be causing inflammation, and 2) visualize my healing.

At the conclusion of each of my meditations, I'd spend an additional 5 minutes visualizing my knee being made whole. I would imagine little worker cells with their trucks and tools working on my knee. With their shovels, they would clear out the damaged tissue. With needles they would sew up my slightly torn meniscus, and then with a hose, they'd add additional cartilage to my knee. I loved visualizing them working on my knee with such love and concern. Then I would imagine myself running with my grandchildren with ease.

I'm still waiting for the physical manifesting of my healing and will continue to add visualization to my meditation until it is completely healed and restored. I'm sure physical therapy and fasting also helped, but together they were a strong combination. Eventually, I decided to get knee surgery, but I'm still grateful that God can provide healing from many different methods and channels.

Use visualization as a powerful practice to enhance your goals, intentions, and desires. No matter what you want to overcome or achieve- low self-esteem, business success, a new home, getting along with your spouse or child, or successfully speaking in front of a crowd, use visualization to bring it forth. See yourself doing what you desire, but not only see it, feel it, experience it inside you, and get excited about it. Visualization can change your life, your relationships, and help you to create our own reality.

At the conclusion of your meditation today, spend 5 extra minutes imagining that you have already received what you are praying or believing God for. You can pick something from your list of affirmations or even your daily declaration. To begin, close your eyes and use your imagination to see, feel, smell, and taste the experience. Try to make your visualization as vivid as possible and see yourself getting really excited about it. Again, mind, body and spirit experts say that the mind doesn't distinguish between perceived or actual reality, so if you're going to daydream be sure to do it with intention.

Later you will write a mission statement and **Faith It Forward Stories**, which are ideal for visualization.

My Meditation Experience. Today's Date _____.

Activity # 1- Checking In - Today I feel...

Activity # 2- My Intention for my date with God is...

Activity # 3– Meditation

I meditated for _____ minutes.

Meditating for me today was…

My thoughts during meditation consisted of…

Meditation helped me to release …

After the meditation, I felt…

Any additional inspirations or messages from God to you?

Activity # 4- Visualization

At the conclusion of your meditation today, spend 5 extra minutes imagining that you have already received what you are praying or believing God for. Record any inspirations or thoughts about your experience.

Psalm 5:3 "In the morning, LORD, you hear my voice; in the morning I lay my requests before you and wait expectantly."

Day 26:
Reflection and Do-Overs

Do you ever have the intention of doing something different, but then defer back to old habits without really even noticing it? In my morning time with God, I would often set an intention to eat healthy foods throughout the day. Then, at work, without really even thinking about it, I'd pick up a cookie or cupcake from the staff lounge and eat it. Sometimes it wasn't until I finished it that I realized I'd "given in" to temptation. This was my old conditioning at play living out my default mental thermostat.

Another technique to help us reprogram our subconscious minds (the mind that we operate under 95% of the time) is to do daily reflections or do-overs. This is a great technique to use at the end of the day. Basically, you just scan your day for anything that you wish you had done differently. Things like snapping at a coworker, getting angry, eating junk food, telling a lie, the list goes on. Next you replay the scene in your mind with a better or more satisfying outcome. Remember the subconscious mind doesn't know what's real or imagined. For example, see yourself saying "no" to the cookie or responding kindly to the co-worker. You can even see your co-worker responding back with a smile or in a kind way as well. If you want, make a whole production out of it. Also, observe yourself getting really excited about making the better choice.

Eventually, in time, you will act out your do-overs in real life as you have practiced them over and over again in your mind. If you have a challenging situation that you face daily, allow reflection and do-overs to help you change your beliefs and actions in these situations.

My Meditation Experience. Today's Date _____.

Activity # 1- Checking In - Today I feel...

Activity # 2- My Intention for my date with God is...

Activity # 3– Meditation

I meditated for _____ minutes.

Meditating for me today was…

My thoughts during meditation consisted of…

Meditation helped me to release …

After the meditation, I felt…

Any additional inspirations or messages from God to you?

Activity # 5- Reflection and Do-Over

Reflect on a recent situation in which you weren't too happy with the outcome. Now in your imagination, practice doing it over with an outcome you'd prefer. Repeat it several times in your mind or even write it down.

Day 27:
Spiritual Journaling

A spiritual journal records your journey towards God. Other than meditation and sacred silence, I can't think of any other practice except reading my Bible that has had a greater impact on my life. I have been journaling for over 15 years. I began spiritual journaling when I was going through a tough time emotionally. Spiritual journaling helped me to work through my pain. During the stillness and quietness of journaling, I was able to hear God's voice comfort and encourage me. It was my time to nurture my spirit and soul, and to pay attention to what I was feeling. Journaling allows you to be real with yourself and to release the hidden treasures of our heart. It can also aid you in self-discovery.

Journaling should be meaningful and rewarding to you. It is not just a chronological diary of the day's events but contains the thoughts, reflections, and perceptions of your daily life and events. It should contain stories, articles, and objects that reflect you and where you want to be spiritually, physically, and mentally. It contains the keepsakes of the heart and soul.

I encourage spiritual journaling after meditation. Once we become still and relaxed, we create a great environment to hear from God and can record any inspiration, visions, or answers God might be giving us, once the meditation ends.

If you are meditating on God's Word or reading an inspirational book, write scriptures, quotes, or excerpts that touch or prick your heart. You can even write prayers and keep a prayer log. The ideas are endless.

You can also engage in what are called **Morning Pages**. I first heard about *Morning Pages* while taking a class called "The Artist Way." *Morning Pages* are another form of journaling where you write 3-pages a day of whatever is showing up in your life. *Morning Pages* enhance creativity, promote healing, increase focus, and clarify your vision. To get started with *Morning Pages,* after meditation, just start writing. Initially it may be difficult trying to think about something to write about for 3-whole pages. If so, you could write about that or any random thoughts that show up. You can also pick something from the journaling prompts on the next page to get you started. Use your *Morning Pages* to also dig deeper into your fears, problems, negative thoughts, and limiting beliefs. *Morning Pages* can also help you to clarify your goals, discover your purpose, tap into your deepest desires, and manifest your vision. By committing to 3-pages, you give yourself both time and permission to go below the surface of your feelings and fears. Bringing awareness to your unconscious beliefs, without judgment, allows for inner healing.

Today, after meditation, in your journal write down any thoughts, inspirations, ideas, or even visions that surfaced in your mind or imagination. Should an exciting thought or idea show up during meditation, "don't" stop meditating. If it's important, you'll remember it. God can use this time to plant new insights or breakthroughs, business ventures, future projects to explore, or ideas to fulfill your passion or purpose. When we begin to clear our minds of the mental and emotional toxins that block our creativity and God's still small voice, we open ourselves to an array of inspiration and possibilities.

Journal Prompts

Past Hurts & Memories	Values & Feelings
1. Think about a time in your life when you felt unworthy. List the details and how you felt. Once you've written these down, close your eyes and invite God into your pain. Envision Christ's love and light dissolving the darkness. Now write about this experience and how you're feeling now. 2. Make a list of three qualities you have that you consider weaknesses, then explore how these so-called weaknesses might be recast as strengths. 3. Think about five qualities of your personality or your outlook that you think defines you. 4. Things I want to let go of… 5. What life events have tainted your heart or stole your peace of mind?	1. If you had to spend a month alone, what 5 books or movies you want to read or watch? What does this say about you? 2. Name three emotions that you'd like to feel everyday? Tell why? What activities can you do regularly to cultivate these feelings? 3. Name three values that you want to live by? What do you need to change in your life to honor them? 4. If you could be anywhere in the world at this very moment, where would you want to be and why? 5. Who are the most important people in your life and why? 6. Write about the main themes and issues showing up in your life.

Vision & Purpose

1. What are some things you need to do to make your dreams come true in the next week, month, or year?
2. What five changes can you make that would bring you more joy?
3. I'm the happiest when…?
4. In detail, describe a perfect day.
5. What risks do you want to take? What's holding you back?
6. What is your top goal? Why is this goal important to you?
7. What new habit would you like to begin this month.
8. What do you need to start saying "yes" to?
9. What are your top desires?

Thoughts & Beliefs

1. What do you fear the most? Why? Is your fear rational?
2. Explore any thought, memory, or emotional sensation that showed up during your meditation time. Keep uncovering the deeper meanings by asking why questions. Also, ask the Holy Spirit to help you go deeper as well. Explore the meanings, beliefs, and agendas to help you dig deeper.
3. Write about something that is frustrating to you.
4. Think about a limiting belief that may be holding you back. Write about where this belief originated and the impact it has had on your life. Rewrite this belief so that it supports your truest desires and values.

Health & Healing

1. How do you feel about your current health? What do you need to focus on most?
2. What activities do you think would make you feel better? Make a plan to carry out those activities.
3. Write about what you perceive to be the worst thing you've ever done. Write about your rationale at the time. Write words of love and forgiveness.
4. What do you need to heal? Really pay attention to what God's Spirit tells you.

Self Esteem

1. Think about a time in your life where you felt unworthy. List the details and how you felt. Once you've written it down, close your eyes and invite God into your pain. Envision Christ's love and light dissolving the darkness. Now write about this experience and how you're feeling now.
2. What qualities about yourself do you love the most?
3. Is there anything you did this week that you wish you'd done differently?
4. What is your biggest struggle with loving yourself.
5. What does your inner critic constantly tell you?

Gratitude	Spirituality
1. How is your life better than it was one, three, or five years ago? 2. Write about your one of your happiest memories? 3. What are your biggest accomplishments? 4. What do you really appreciate about your life? 5. What have you learned or what information have you received that you are grateful for? 6. Think about your life. What has it given you that you have taken granted for?	1. What speaks to you on a spiritual level? 2. What does it mean to be a "spiritual person"? What behaviors do you associate with being spiritual? 3. What does it mean to *grow* spiritually and how do you know if you have grown? 4. If you were to focus more on growing spiritually, what changes would you need to make in your life? What would you give up, if anything, and what would you need to do more of?

My Meditation Experience. Today's Date _____.

Activity # 1- Checking In - Today I feel...

Activity # 2- My Intention for my date with God is...

Activity # 3– Meditation

I meditated for _____ minutes.

Meditating for me today was...

My thoughts during meditation consisted of…

Meditation helped me to release …

After the meditation, I felt…

Any additional inspirations or messages from God to you?

Activity # 4- Spiritual Journaling

Spend 10 minutes (or longer) writing down any thoughts, inspirations, or ideas that surfaced during or after your meditation time. If you want to take the challenge, start writing *Morning Pages.* Use the prompts, if needed, to get you started.

Jeremiah 30:2 "Thus says the Lord, the God of Israel: Write in a book all the words that I have spoken to you."

Day 28:
Faith It Forward Story

You can also create a **Faith It Forward** story each month or anytime you want to believe God for something new in your life.

A *Faith It Forward* story is a narrative you write that describes how your month or an event will turn out before it happens. It's like writing a news story announcing the outcome BEFORE it takes place.

This is very powerful because its laser focuses your mind and intentions on what you really want to accomplish in full detail.

The scripture says that we walk by faith and not by sight (2 Corinthians 5:7) and without faith, it is impossible to please God (Hebrews 11:6). Could it be that God is not working in our lives because we haven't given Him much with which to work?

James 4: 2 tells us, *"You have not because you ask not."* Mark 11:24 declares, *"Whatever you ask for in prayer when you ask, ask in faith believing that you have already received it and it will be yours."* I believe God wants us to ask for what we want and then thank Him for the outcome.

In fact, Hebrews 11:6 says, *"And without faith, it is impossible to please God because anyone who comes to Him must believe that He exists and that He rewards those who earnestly seek Him."*

Several years ago, I used *Faith It Forward* to sell my rental home. My wonderful tenant suddenly died, and his grown but immature adult children temporarily moved in. It was almost like living in a nightmarish dream.

Shortly after putting the house on the market, I made a flier on my computer. The flier included a picture of the house with a big SOLD sign on it that I taped to my refrigerator door. Each time I passed by it, I thanked God for selling my home. I also wrote a short story regarding its sale in my journal. In my story, I wrote about all the buyers who loved my home and made great offers. Then, I would read it aloud several times per week. I could hardly believe it, when the house sold despite a myriad of issues. I honestly contributed its sale to keeping my words, thoughts, and attitude aligned with faith and a vision of what I wanted to happen.

Several years ago, I created a *Faith It Forward* story regarding healing for my daughter and grandson. I read these every day along with one of the daily declarations. Here is an example of what I wrote in my journal:

By Jesus Stripes, They Were Healed

God is still in the healing business! My daughter Jessica was healed from chronic headaches, shoulder, and neck pain. God healed her and restored her to perfect health, and she gives Him all the glory. Praise the Lord.

When we got the MRI test back from the doctor regarding Tyler's knee, the MRI was completely normal. No torn ligament, no bone chip! He was completely healed. The doctor called it a miracle; I called it God's healing power. Amen.

Maybe you want a new job, to meet the man or woman of your dreams, to have more confidence, greater appreciation, or even a better relationship with your parents. Whatever it is, write a *Faith It Forward* story illustrating exactly what you want with the positive outcomes. I recommend writing a new story at the beginning of each month and reading it several times per week. Reading it often will keep it fresh in your mind.

When dealing with fear, doubt or resistance, you can use the *Welcoming* and *Putting Off Prayer*, to restore your faith and enthusiasm (in upcoming lessons). Also, don't worry about when or how it will happen. Leave that up to God. Just keep your heart free from worry, fear, or doubt, and God will do the rest.

My Meditation Experience. Today's Date _____.

Activity # 1- Checking In - Today I feel…

Activity # 2- My Intention for my date with God is…

Activity # 3– Meditation

I meditated for _____ minutes.

Meditating for me today was…

My thoughts during meditation consisted of…

Meditation helped me to release …

After the meditation, I felt…

Any additional inspirations or messages from God to you?

Activity # 5- Faith It Forward Story

Write a *Faith It Forward* story for something that you want to manifest or write one for the upcoming month. Write it in the affirmative as if it has already happened by adding lots of details, even the comments of others. Read it as often as possible and squelch all fear and doubt that arises.

Proverbs 4:25 "Let
your eyes look
directly forward, and
your gaze be straight
before you."

Day 29:
Discovering Silence

One of the truest gifts for a busy life is an extended period of silence; a time when we intentionally turn our attention away from the rush of conversations and commitments, images and messages, lists and obligations, and quietly attune ourselves to our inner space. For some of us, imposed silence has been a punishment in our past; for example, a parent may have admonished, "Close your mouth and go to your room."

The silence we are entering here is a choice. This silence is a chance for discovery to find out new and different things. The absence of talk is quite different when we are choosing not to speak. Silence is not a lack of communication. There is a subtle language that connects us to one another through the eyes, with a smile, or a gesture. Fluency in this subtle language calls for our ability to observe the small details of life. As we develop our faculties with this subtle language, we find that we are less dependent on the mechanical devices that can connect us, but that can also make us feel more separate.

In moving into an inner space of silence, we are attuning ourselves to the spirit of nature and letting go of the tendency to be critical. Silence provides the opportunity for me to identify the qualities in myself that have the capacity to transform me. In silence, I can connect to the highest quality of my lightest, clearest thinking.

Action emerges from the seeds of thought. Actions are the fruits of these seeds. What is the soil in which I choose to plant the seeds of my thoughts? Violence or peace? Anger or love? These choices are transformative. The state of awareness I attain in silence connects directly to the quality of my understanding. Understanding "in sound" is a cognitive process, while understanding "in silence" is subtler, resulting in realizations that emerge from within. These are very different experiences.

In silence, I discover my innate qualities, the qualities that are intrinsic to who I am. Here in silence, I touch my eternal self, and I come to trust this deepest essence. The experience of recognizing my intrinsic and unique qualities increases my own power to receive. In silence, I touch my inner strength and experience trust, faith, safety, beauty, and worthiness. It is from this base of inner strength that my actions evolve. In silence, I can listen to the call of God, the call of nature, and the call of others in need.

Silence is an inner space of learning. When I do not understand something, I continue to hold on to it. When learning has occurred, I can release it and move on. In silence, I discover truth by getting in touch with my true self and God. Silence increases my capacity to hold the truth within. Silence is an opportunity to rest in the lap of my own greatness. Remember to care for yourself with the special attention you would accord any great soul. Silence is a discipline, not of doing, but of being.

My Meditation Experience. Today's Date _____.

Activity # 1- Checking In - Today I feel...

Activity # 2- My Intention for my date with God is...

Activity # 3– Meditation

I meditated for _____ minutes.

Meditating for me today was...

My thoughts during meditation consisted of...

Meditation helped me to release ...

After the meditation, I felt…

Any additional inspirations or messages from God to you?

Activity # 4- Discovering Silence

After the meditation, reset your timer for 10 minutes and just sit in silence, no music or distractions, just plain silence. You can even focus on an item in the room to help anchor your mind. Silence is not only the absence of sound but also the absence of thought. Notice the thoughts or other visual distractions, but then return back to experiencing the silence. Record in your journal what this experience was like for you. Make spending time in silence, both sitting in a chair, lying on the ground, or even in nature a part of life.

Psalm 62:5 "For God alone, O my soul, wait in silence, for my hope is from him."

inner
healing

Inner Healing

Day 30:
Negative Self Talk

It was Christian meditation integrated with the scriptures that helped me overcome 4 years of a deep depression. I remember so clearly the day my healing began. I was waiting for my kids to get out of school. I sat there in my green minivan wrenched with emotional pain so thick you could cut it with a knife. As I waited, I began to take deep breaths and with each exhalation, I would mentally affirm, "I release pain."

Within 10 minutes the pain was gone, and I experienced a peace that had alluded me for very long. As I dwelled in the quiet, the spirit of God spoke to my heart. In a still, small voice, He said, "Rhonda, the reason you are so depressed is because of the thoughts you are thinking." Prior to this, I wasn't paying much attention to my thoughts, but now aware of them, I listened. They came faster than a parading machine gun and they were destructive, debilitating, and downright mean. Every day, I was beating myself down. I was saying words to myself that I'd never let another person get away with. Yet they were able to sneak into my sub-conscious mind day after day. Over the next few months, I learned that by changing my negative self-talk, I could change my perspective and alleviate my mood.

From that day on I made a conscious effort to stop these negative thoughts and alter my thinking. It wasn't an easy thing because our thoughts become a part of who we are, but I was determined. After several months of examining and prohibiting negative thoughts from entering my mental garden, my depression lifted. Now some 10 years later, I share my story with my Christian brothers and sisters so they can enjoy deliverance as well.

Depression has many causes. It can be biological or psychological. Biological factors that contribute to depression are side effects of medication, physical illness, hormonal changes, or other neurochemical disorders. Psychological factors, which are the most common reasons for depression, include interpersonal losses (loss of a loved one), external losses (loss of a job), unfortunate life events, physical disease, and prolonged stress.

When faced with traumatic or painful events, there are many ways we can respond. If we acknowledge our pain and losses and allow the healing process to take place, we eventually move past the pain into acceptance and well-being.

However, depression often results when we deny or suppress our painful feelings, instead of working through and releasing them. As Christians, we may believe being strong or not showing true emotions is a sign of strength or faith. Yet, research shows that it takes anywhere from 2 to 10 years to recover from the loss or death of a loved one. Therefore, we must give ourselves permission to grieve. What we repress or resist persist and begins to affect us on a subconscious level, often resulting in depression or other toxic emotions.

People who live through difficult situations or losses successfully tend to do the following actions: 1) they accept their painful feelings as normal, 2) they give themselves permission to feel their painful emotions, 3) they allow themselves to express their feelings, 4) they stay in contact with supportive family and friends, 5) they engage in problem solving, and lastly, 6) they maintain a clear view of reality.

It is number 6, not "maintaining a clear view of reality" that catapults many people into a spiraling depression. Instead of perceiving negative events as they truly are and working through them in a healthy process, those most susceptible to depression begin to interpret events in the most negative light. Their thoughts become distorted; they make erroneous predictions, jump to conclusions, engage in all-or-none thinking, have tunnel vision, personalize situations, and insist that things should be a certain way.

According to John Preston, Psy.D. and author of *You Can Beat Depression: A Guide to Recovery*, "Distortions or errors in thinking and perceiving are seen in almost all types of depression. As a person begins to feel depressed, thoughts and perceptions become extremely negative and pessimistic. Such distortions not only are a symptom of depression but also are a major cause of depression, and in fact, are probably the most potent factor that prolongs and intensifies depression," stated Preston.

Although those who are depressed engage in all these types of destructive thinking, much of it is unconscious to them. "Many times, people are not aware of the inner thinking that occurs during times of emotional pain," said Preston. "An important and effective method of becoming aware of cognitions (our thoughts) involves using feelings as signals or cues." For example, "As soon as you notice such a feeling- sadness or frustration- use this emotion to let you know, 'Ok, something is going on in my mind.' Then ask yourself one or more of the following questions:"

"What Is Going Through My Mind Right Now?"

"What Am I Thinking?"

"What Am I Telling Myself?"

"What Am I Perceiving About the Situation That Triggered This Feeling?"

It is difficult to change your emotions without first recognizing the thoughts behind them. Once you are paying attention to your thinking, you can alter your thoughts and bring them into reality or under the authority of Christ.

If you are depressed or suffering from other toxic emotions, I encourage you to keep a journal for several days recording each of your thoughts. For reoccurring thoughts, just put a tally next to the phrase every time you think it.

The next step is to begin to challenge every thought that is contrary to God's word or that is distorted or unrealistic. Thoughts like, "I'll never find another job, no one will ever love me again, everybody hates me, I'm the loneliest person on earth, I can't do anything right, I'm never going to feel happy again, or he shouldn't have left me" are examples of distorted thoughts not based in reality.

Now that you have your thoughts listed on paper, it's time to alter or modify these erroneous thoughts and make them healthier and more realistic. On a sheet of paper, list your distorted thoughts on the left side and draw a line down the middle. On the right side, you will challenge each negative thought with a realistic response. For example:

"I'll never find another job" may be responded with, "I can't see into the future, but God said He will meet all my needs. I am going to do a better job of trusting Him."

"No one will ever love me again" may be responded with, "I know that I feel disappointed with this loss, but that doesn't mean that God doesn't have someone else special just for me."

"Everybody hates me" may be responded with, "Maybe this person doesn't like me, but I know I am a good person, and I do have many friends and family members who do love me."

Continue to do this with each negative thought you listed and then continue to challenge each negative thought with rational ones or scriptures. If you can't do it alone, ask a friend to help you come up with rational responses. As you continue to do this, just like me, your depression will begin to subside.

In addition to challenging my thoughts, faith-based meditation helped me to continually observe my thinking and learn to control thoughts by letting them go. Christian meditation along with thought therapy can help you gain back your peace and joy.

If you have a difficult time implementing these techniques, don't hesitate to contact a Christian counselor who believes in meditation and cognitive therapy. Sometimes you need the extra support and accountability that a professional or group provides. Even if you are prescribed medication, it's still a good idea to work on your thought processes. Whatever the case, you can be healed from depression. I am living proof.

My Meditation Experience. Today's Date _____.

Activity # 1- Checking In - Today I feel...

Activity # 2- My Intention for my date with God is...

Activity # 3– Meditation

I meditated for _____ minutes.

Meditating for me today was...

My thoughts during meditation consisted of...

Meditation helped me to release ...

After the meditation I felt…

Any additional inspirations or messages from God to you?

Activity # 5- Negative Self Talk

Today, spend an hour or two through-out the day monitoring your self-talk. On a sheet of paper, begin to write down your reoccurring negative thoughts. Use this awareness to combat these thoughts by doing the assignment for this day (on the right side of the paper write your counterargument). Another technique is to just say "Stop" to each negative thought as it shows up. In the beginning, you may be saying "Stop" in your mind quite often. Try to continue this throughout the week. If you do, you'll notice that the thoughts begin to slow down and eventually subside.

Matthew 12:35 "A good man brings good things out of the good stored up in him,"

Day 31:
What You Can Feel You Can Heal #2

When it comes to our emotions, so many of us play the avoidance game. We deny how we feel, cover it up, or sweep them under the rug. We tell ourselves that "we shouldn't feel this way," and continue to bury our pain and hurt instead of dealing with it head-on.

I understand that it can be painful digging up hurtful memories or addressing our pain. It's almost like pulling the band-aid off of a wound that has never fully healed. However, when we don't deal with our wounds, it's just a matter of time before something or someone rips off that band-aid and the emotions flare.

God doesn't want us to hide our pain but to heal it, and that starts with first acknowledging it and then feeling it. You'll learn in the Welcoming Prayer (upcoming lesson) that our emotions don't show up to torment us, but to show us the areas we need healing so that we can offer them up to God and bring His light into our pain.

What we can feel, we can heal. I remember many years ago when I was suffering from extreme pain and loneliness. For months I had involved myself in a myriad of activities to keep me busy so that I could avoid the emptiness and anxiety inside of me. Eventually, I got tired of running. One day I was sitting home alone in the silence and it literally felt like the walls were closing in on me. All I could do was lay down and hold myself tightly in a fetal position.

I felt the pain swelling up within me getting hotter and hotter. I thought I would go crazy. Then an interesting thing happened. The pain began to subside.

It was like it had burned right through me. At that moment, something in me changed. I had faced my fears and feelings and survived. That moment changed my life. I no longer feared my emotions because I knew they really couldn't hurt me. From then on, I stopped suppressing my pain with distractions and learned the techniques I'll share with you in this section- to acknowledge your feelings by giving them a voice which will then allow them to go free.

One more thing, the only way to release and let go of your stuff is to heal it first. Once it is healed, it will naturally fall from your life.

My Meditation Experience. Today's Date _____.

Activity # 1- Checking In - Today I feel...

Activity # 2- My Intention for my date with God is...

Activity # 3– Meditation

I meditated for _____ minutes.
Meditating for me today was...

My thoughts during meditation consisted of...

Meditation helped me to release ...

After the meditation, I felt...

Any additional inspirations or messages from God to you?

Activity # 4- What You Can Feel You Can Heal

Take a moment to reflect on any past pains or hurts that have not been fully healed in your life. How do you know you're not healed? Your emotions flair by the words or actions of others or when trigged by certain events. Write about it and share your hurt with God. You'll use some of the techniques in the coming days to help you begin the healing process of letting it go.

Psalms 34:18 "The
LORD is close to the
brokenhearted and
saves those who are
crushed in spirit."

Day 32:
Putting Off Prayer

Think about the problem, concern, or situation that you want God to heal in your life? Are you ready to release it to God and let it go? Before Jesus healed anyone, he asked him or her, *"Do you want to be healed?"* You would think this would be obvious, but when we live with pain or dysfunction long enough, it becomes part of our identity and we may have a hard time letting it go.

Did you know that our bodies hold unto emotions at a cellular level and if not eradicated, can often manifest as disease in the body? In fact, dis-ease, illness, or pain in various organs can relate to specific types of emotions. For example, the liver is associated with anger. People with Chronic Fatigue Syndrome may harbor negative or hateful feelings towards themselves. Even the CDC and the World Health Organization state on their website that 80-85% of all illness has an emotional root! If that is the case, what do we need to work on!

During my retreats, I talk about the healing ladder. The healing ladder shows the progression of how healing takes place. It begins at the mind and moves up the ladder until we reach bliss. However, many ill people try to fix their bodies, but they may need to start with their minds and emotions first!

It's important that we look for the root cause of our pain, but that's not always possible. Some of our hurts happened long ago or plague us at a subconscious level. Even so, we can address them and heal them. The **Putting Off and Putting On Prayer** is one tool to do this.

The **Putting Off and Putting On Prayer** allows you to recognize and release or detach from toxic feelings instead of making them your own.

Today, you're going to use the **Putting Off and Putting On Prayer** to cleanse your mind and purify your heart to let go of toxic feelings as well as to destroy the fiery darts of the enemy whose sole purpose is to kill your vision, steal your joy, and destroy your testimony.

Let's start with some basics:
Negative Emotions to Put OFF: fear, anger, pride, jealousy, hopelessness, insecurity, hatred, anxiety, restlessness, condemnation, guilt, shame, doubt, worry, unforgiveness, greed, lust, rage, selfishness, bitterness, meanness, laziness, slothfulness, lying, deceit, etc.

Colossians 3: 5-10 – "Put to (put off) death, therefore, whatever belongs to your earthly nature: sexual immorality, impurity, lust, evil desires and greed, which is idolatry. Because of these, the wrath of God is coming. You used to walk in these ways, in the life you once lived. But now you must also rid yourselves of all such things as these: anger, rage, malice, slander, and filthy language from your lips. Do not lie to each other, since you have taken off your old self with its practices and have put on the new self, which is being renewed in the knowledge in the image of its Creator."

Positive Emotions to Put ON: love, joy, peace, longsuffering, patience, wisdom, trust, hope, faith, forgiveness, generosity, compassion, kindness, gratitude, self-love, self-acceptance, power, humility, thankfulness, honesty, integrity, etc.

Colossians 3:12-15: "Therefore, as God's chosen people, holy and dearly loved, clothe yourselves (put on) with compassion, kindness, humility, gentleness, and patience. Bear with each other and forgive one another if any of you has a grievance against someone. Forgive as the Lord forgave you. And over all these virtues put on love, which binds them all together in perfect unity. Let the peace of Christ rule in your hearts, since as members of one body you were called to peace. And be thankful."

Make Your List

Find the list of emotions or behaviors that you recorded in your journal that are contaminating your body and spirit. One at a time, read aloud using the prayer below. You can also add behaviors as well. Read through the prayer once before starting. Replace your specific emotion or behavior where indicated. You'll also need a new emotion to replace it with.

Read the **Putting Off and Putting On Prayer** one time before beginning, then begin reading the prayer with your list.

As you go through this prayer, any time you feel any strong sensations in your body, pause, and take a few deep breaths, then continue.

"**Name the negative emotion** you are not from God. I don't want you. You have no place in my life. Father search my heart, search through every aspect of my being, through every cell of my body, to the very root and core of <u>negative emotion</u> and remove it.

I, by your grace, accept the courage to forgive myself, to forgive others, to forgive every circumstance that has contributed to the feelings and manifestation of <u>negative emotion</u> in my life. Now <u>negative emotion,</u> I send you away. I bind you from my heart and my innermost being in the mighty name of Jesus. Jesus, I thank you for setting me free, now!

In the name of Jesus, I choose to put on **name the new emotion you want to feel or experience**. I am in Christ. I accept God's unconditional love for me. I deeply and completely love and accept myself as well. The <u>new emotion</u> of Christ abounds in my heart. I choose to feel <u>new emotion,</u> now. I choose to speak <u>new emotion,</u> now. And by the grace of God, I trust the <u>new emotion</u> of God to manifest in my life, now. I declare that ALL things are working together for my highest good because God is in absolute control. Amen! Glory to God!"

My Meditation Experience. Today's Date _____.

Activity # 1- Checking In - Today I feel…

Activity # 2- My Intention for my date with God is…

Activity # 3– Meditation

I meditated for _____ minutes.

Meditating for me today was…

My thoughts during meditation consisted of…

Meditation helped me to release …

After the meditation, I felt…

Any additional inspirations or messages from God to you?

Activity # 4- Putting It Off Prayer
The **Putting Off Prayer** is great for combatting spiritual warfare and those times when you are struggling with uncomfortable emotions brought on by fear. If you are dealing with any recent anxiety, depression, fear, or any other toxic emotion, use the putting off prayer to dissolve them. Repeat as necessary.

Day 33:
Welcoming Prayer

Working Through Strongholds and Toxic Emotions

No matter how much meditating, scripture reading, or journaling that you do, there are just going to be those days that you feel like crap! Maybe you have lost your job, have major financial woes, your relationship ended, you got another bad diagnosis, your child got suspended from school, and no matter what you do, there is a heavy dark cloud following you around and raining on top of your head. This is another reason a date with God is so powerful. You don't have to just settle for feeling bad all day, week, or month. You can take charge of your mind and emotions and take the necessary steps to restore your wellbeing and peace of mind. However, the more diligent you are with spending time with God, the less these situations will affect you. Your trust in God and His presence in your life will take up the slack and leave you feeling at peace when you might otherwise be 'freaking out.' God does promise us peace that passes all understanding, but that peace only comes about by abiding closely and continuously with Him (Philippians 4:6-7).

In this section, I want to introduce you to *The Welcoming Prayer.* This prayer is used to eliminate toxic thoughts, emotions, and sensations that come suddenly and overwhelm you. You will not do the *Welcoming Prayer* every day, but it is in your toolbox whenever you need it.

Another tool for restoring mental and emotional health and wellness that I recommend is EFT or Emotional Freedom Technique. I do a Christian version of EFT on my YouTube channel at _http://www.youtube.com/thechristianmeditato (yes, the "r" is missing.) But let me get back to *The Welcoming Prayer.*

What is the Welcoming Prayer?
The Welcoming Prayer originated with Mary Mrozowski, a Catholic woman who wanted to help people overcome toxic thoughts and emotions. Around 2012, I attended a weekend retreat on *The Welcoming Prayer* and found it very useful for dealing with sudden disturbing emotions.

I want to begin by having you read the poem *The Guest House* by Rumi:

This being human is a guest house.
Every morning a new arrival.
A joy, a depression, a meanness,
some momentary awareness comes
as an unexpected visitor.
Welcome and entertain them all!
Even if they're a crowd of sorrows,
who violently sweep your house
empty of its furniture,
still, treat each guest honorably.
He may be clearing you out
for some new delight.
The dark thought, the shame, the malice,
meet them at the door laughing,
and invite them in.
Be grateful for whoever comes,
because each has been sent
as a guide from beyond.

I absolutely love this poem. It's telling us to be thankful for the emotions we experience. Why be thankful? Well, our emotions give us valuable clues about our state of mind and teach us something about ourselves. They also come to offer us healing and allows us to turn these feelings and emotions over to our Creator. When we continue to do so, God transforms us from within.

The Bible tells us that the fruit of the Spirit is love, joy, peace, longsuffering, and the like (Galatians 5:22-23).

If you're a human being, even if you are saved, sanctified, and filled with the Holy Ghost, there are those days you'd have to look long and hard before you'd find peace anywhere in your surroundings. This lack of peace is letting you know that God's Spirit is not operating in your life at the moment. It is like a flashing warning sign saying "intruder! intruder! intruder!" At that moment, you have many options. You can let that worry continue to spiral out of control and completely overtake your life or you can do whatever is necessary (and legal) to get that villain out and get God's peace and spirit operating back into your life.

Emotions like anger, worry, depression, jealousy, judgment, resentment, self-pity, and envy are letting you know that you've been taken hostage by an ungodly entity that is stealing God's fruit from your mental, emotional, and spiritual tree. And no, I don't mean a demon has possessed you.

The Welcoming Prayer, which I will share momentarily, helps us cope with issues that suddenly come up in our daily lives. Christ wants to heal our emotional programs (default or unconscious mindsets and behaviors), but we must consent to let Him do so. Through consent, we open our hearts to healing and transformation, without trying to control the situation or the outcome.

As we maneuver through life, we continue to try and get our needs met in the same old subconscious ways. Choosing new and alternative methods to react to circumstances releases us from being a victim of our patterns and emotions. Afflicted and toxic emotions are lethal to our well-being. When we suppress our emotions, we're turning them inward, on ourselves. When we act out our frustration, we can become hurtful and harmful to others.

The Welcoming Prayer opens the way for us to dis-identify with our emotional program for happiness, meaning that, all too often, we seek happiness down the wrong paths. *The Welcoming Prayer* opens the door to spaciousness, the ability to see from a new perspective and to be proactive instead of reactive.

Read *the Welcoming Prayer* by Mary Mrozowski below:

> *Welcome, welcome, welcome.*
> *I welcome everything that comes to me in this moment*
> *because I know it is for my healing.*
> *I welcome all thoughts, feelings, emotions,*
> *persons, situations, and conditions.*
> *Welcome, welcome.*
> *I let go of my desire for security.*
> *I let go of my desire for approval.*
> *I let go of my desire for control.*
> *I let go of my desire to change any*
> *situation, condition, person, or myself.*
> *I open to the love and presence of God*
> *and the healing action and grace within.*

As you can see, *The Welcoming Prayer* is our consent to acknowledge what we are feeling and then surrender it to the healing power of God. There are four steps to using this prayer.

Step One: Focus and feel where you are feeling the emotion in your body. Zero in on particular feelings, emotions, body sensations, thoughts, or mental commentary. Breathe into this spot. If you can, identify the emotion. If not, don't worry about it, just acknowledge and feel the sensation as fully as possible. You may feel:

- Tenseness in your shoulders
- Shortness of breath
- Shaking, all over
- Upset stomach
- Shallow breathing
- Adrenaline or anxiety
- Excited or nauseated
- Chest pain
- Increased heart rate
- Heightened awareness

These feelings don't come from our brain but from our subconscious. Greet the sensation, or emotion, with love. Instead of resisting it or trying to make it go away, embrace it fully. This is how you are feeling at the moment, regardless of how irrational. It is important to really experience the sensation in the body and not rush through it.

Imagine the analogy of a small child who keeps coming for attention, and a parent who keeps brushing him or her way. The child begins to clamor for the parent's attention or gets louder. If the parent would just stop and acknowledge the child, then he or she would be satisfied and leave. Greet the sensation in the same manner. Denying our feelings keeps them unconsciously alive.

Step Two: Once you have accepted it, begin to repeat *The Welcoming Prayer* slowly in your mind, or read it if you haven't memorized it, which I do recommend.

Step Three: Take in a deep breath and let it go. You are letting go of your need for security, approval, control, and your desire to change the emotion, the circumstance or the persons involved. Instead, you are opening your heart to God's presence and His healing action that will spring forth from within.

Step Four: Don't get trapped in expectations. You may not always see immediate gratification, but that doesn't mean it's not working. Just continue with the process and let God do the work of transformation. This doesn't mean we don't need to change things, but to change from a place of wholeness and healing, and not of fear or desperation. Therefore, let go of the desire to change what you are experiencing in the present moment.

My Meditation Experience. Today's Date _____.

Activity # 1- Checking In - Today I feel...

Activity # 2- My Intention for my date with God is...

Activity # 3– Meditation

I meditated for _____ minutes.

Meditating for me today was...

My thoughts during meditation consisted of...

Meditation helped me to release …

After the meditation, I felt…

Any additional inspirations or messages from God to you?

Activity # 4- Welcoming Prayer

In the Feel It, Heal It #1 Section, you recorded a painful hurt or memory that still plagues you from time to time. Today, use the *Welcoming Prayer* to begin the healing process. Don't worry if it's not completely gone after one-go-round. Continue to use it each time the emotion visits you. See it knocking at your door saying, "I'm ready to be healed a little more today." Welcome it in and feel it as you allow God's healing light to enter into your pain.

passing
the
baton

Passing the Baton

Day 34:
Follow Your Heart- Let the Spirit Guide Your Routine

Our relationship with God is not a cookie-cutter or one-program fits all. The *Christian Meditation Journal* provides you with a template (skeleton) that you can shape, create, or modify in any way you want, to draw closer to God and heal your life. Although each part of the body is important, we all have unique and different functions and purposes. Therefore, what is best for you may not be best for someone else. Besides, our lives go through many seasons and transitions and we need different supports during these times.

Our time with God is no different. In everything, we should be guided by the Holy Spirit within, who knows what we need before we even ask. The Spirit knows the intricate and deep things of God and it knows us as well.

My date with God changes as I change, and sometimes daily. Some days I need inner healing, so I'll incorporate the *Welcoming or Putting Off Prayer*. Other days I need to pour out my heart to God through journaling. Then there are times when I have a need or desire and I'll write a *Faith It Forward* story and read it for the week.

The one thing I try to do consistently is the **Basics**, which includes: Checking in, setting an intention, and meditation. These are the three daily spiritual supplements that help keep me mentally, emotionally, and spiritually healthy and grounded in Christ. These spiritual disciplines help me stay connected to God as my source as well as my own heart.

My time with God is my daily ritual to keep my mind and heart pure, stay emotionally balanced, and a time to work through any toxic thoughts or emotions that would steal my peace of mind and joy, causing me to be less effective in my life.

My Meditation Experience. Today's Date _____.

Activity # 1- Checking In - Today I feel…

Activity # 2- My Intention for my date with God is…

Activity # 3– Meditation

I meditated for _____ minutes.

Meditating for me today was…

My thoughts during meditation consisted of…

Meditation helped me to release …

After the meditation, I felt…

Any additional inspirations or messages from God to you?

Activity # 4- Be Your Own Guide

Today, you will select 2 or 3 of the **Beyond the Basics** spiritual disciplines that are resonating with you at this time in your life. Once you identify, write a short paragraph on each, stating how you believe you can benefit from them and why. If you'd like to see an article and video on my 20-minute routine (the one at the time), go to or click here: https://thechristianmeditator.com/20-minute-biblical-morning-routine/

Day 35:
On Your Own with God

Congrats! You have completed what makes up the four components of my *Christian Meditation Journal:* The foundation, the basics, beyond the basics, and inner healing. Now you are ready to navigate your own date with God and you've learned many tools and spiritual disciplines to help you.

To get started, I first recommend deciding how much time you can devote to your time with God each day and protect this valuable time. Always remember that anytime that we devote to God will be given back to us multiplied, the Bible says pressed down, shaken together, and running over. We can't out-give God.

Also, starting each day with God at the helm, and incorporating His peace, guidance, and wisdom in your life, will help you to work more productively and with fewer internal distractions. Instead of spending your day worrying, during your quiet time cast your cares and burdens on God, find inner healing, and start each day refreshed and renewed.

Your date with God is like a shower of the mind and heart. It's where we come to reset our day and die daily to the things of this world and the distractions and desires that pull us in so many different directions. Your time with God will help you to work smarter and not harder. Yes, all this can be done in just 20 minutes a day.

I encourage you to keep it going and discover the benefits of a regular and consistent meditation practice. Start with the basics and add what you need when you need it. Use Today's Inspirations to record your inner thoughts and knowings on a daily. Use this time to get to know yourself and God more fully.

Once you've developed a real habit, missing your time with God and meditation will leave a void in your heart. Your spirit craves to be united with God and in His presence- the secret place.

Once you've established your morning routine, consider adding an evening quiet time to close out your day to let go of any cares or spiritual toxins that might have attached to you throughout the day. This will help you sleep better at night.

Once you're consistent in keeping your meditation routine, check out my book, *"Detox Your Life & Awaken Your Inner Spirit,"* or my upcoming journal, *"Design your Day, Design Your Life."* Instead of creating a meditation routine, you'll partake in fun daily practices and disciplines to help you recreate your life and manifest your desires.

Always Remember- "Your Strength Is in Your Routine!"

Also, if you are enjoying this journal, please leave positive feedback on Amazon and email me regarding your progress or even a testimony. I'd love to hear from you.

FYI- The *Christian Meditation Journal Entries Book* #2 contains additional journal entries that can be purchased and used to continue your daily time with God and journaling practice, if desired. You can order a copy at https://christianmeditationjournal.com.

My Meditation Experience. Today's Date _____.

Activity # 1- Checking In - Today I feel...

Activity # 2- My Intention for my date with God is...

Activity # 3– Meditation

I meditated for _____ minutes.

Meditating for me today was...

My thoughts during meditation consisted of...

Meditation helped me to release …

After the meditation, I felt…

Any additional inspirations or messages from God to you?

Activity # 4- Keeping It Going

Write down your commitment to keeping your date with God going. Record the days and times of your appointment and what you plan to do to keep distractions at bay. Now that you don't have daily commentary, you may be thinking, okay, I'm done with this process, time to move onto something else. In reality, there really is anything else. When you draw closer to God, He will provide all that you need. You can stop searching and continue to seek God for everything that you need. He will add it to you as you keep your eyes, mind, and heart on Him and continue to purify your heart from all that may stand in the way of His divine light and purpose operating in your life.

Proverbs 4:25 "Let
your eyes look
directly forward, and
your gaze be straight
before you."

appendix

Philippians 4:8 "Finally, brothers and sisters, whatever is true, whatever is noble, whatever is right, whatever is pure, whatever is pure, whatever is lovely, whatever is admirable — if anything is excellent or praiseworthy — think about such things."

Appendix

More Daily Declarations

Daily Declaration #1: Guidance and Direction

I declare that I am led and guided by the Holy Spirit. I seek first the kingdom of God and everything I need is added unto me. I trust God with all my heart and lean not to my own understanding. In all my ways I acknowledge Him, and He directs my steps. Because God is for me, He's more than the whole world against me. I wait upon the Lord. God will never leave me or forsake me. I can say with confidence; the Lord is my helper; I will not fear what man can do to me. I am one with God, mind, body, and spirit. My steps are ordered by the Lord. This is my declaration. Amen!

Daily Declaration #2: Loving Yourself

I declare that I am worthy of love and appreciation. The love I feel for myself radiates to those around me. I am living in a place I love, with people who love and appreciate me. I pamper and nurture myself every chance I get. I am committed to loving myself first. I set healthy boundaries for myself. I am valuable. I am worthy. I am real and authentic. I am lovable. I release the need to be someone I am not. I say what I feel, with tact and kindness. People want to hear what I have to say. I remove all masks and barriers that hide who I really am. I release the need to put myself down. I am AWESOME. I am God's child and made in His image. I release the need to prove myself to anyone. The love and light of God fills my entire being. I see all people through the eyes of love. I deeply and completely love and accept myself. I love being me. I am comfortable with who I am. I am the love that I seek. I give love and it's reflected back to me. I am free to be the real me. I am a divine presence in the family of God. This is my declaration. Amen!

Daily Declaration #3: Health and Wellness

I declare that I am healthy and whole, in mind, body, and spirit. By Jesus stripes, I have been healed. My body is the temple of the Holy Spirit and I treat my body with the utmost care. I only put healthy and nutritious foods in my body. I say 'no' to unhealthy food choices, especially sugar, white flour, and processed foods. I exercise my body regularly.

I take the time to love and nurture myself because I am worth the effort. I make an effort to keep my life in perfect balance. My body is healed. My mind is healed. My emotions are healed. I am full of energy. I am full of vitality.

I am thankful for my total health, healing, and well-being. Every assignment of evil against me is defeated. I bind from my heart and mind every spirit of depression, oppression, hopelessness, doubt, and negativity, and I command them to leave my presence at once, in the name of Jesus. I walk in power and victory. This is my declaration. Amen!

Daily Declaration #4: Abundance and Success

I declare that everything I need to succeed comes my way. There is more than enough for me and all who desire abundance. Every area of my life is lining up to God's divine purpose and plan for me. I am abundantly blessed in my business, my finances, and my relationships. Money comes to me easily and effortlessly. Doors of opportunity open up all around me. I say YES to abundance and prosperity. God is guiding my footsteps to success. I don't work harder, I work smarter. I speak those things that are not as those they already were. God is doing exceedingly abundantly above what I can imagine, ask for, or think. I attract abundance from multiple income streams and sources. I am prospering every day in every way. I am thriving and loving every minute of it. Good things are ALWAYS happening to me. God's blessings are overtaking me. God is my source and supply. This is my declaration. Amen!

Daily Declaration #5: Sound Mind

I declare that all my thoughts are good, loving, kind, positive, and focused. I squash all negative thoughts immediately. I seek God's loving and transformative presence more than anything else I know. I take everything to God in prayer. I am led by the Spirit because I have the mind of Christ. Every assignment of evil against me is defeated. I bind from my heart and mind every spirit of depression, oppression, hopelessness, doubt, and negativity, and I command them to leave my presence at once, in the name of Jesus. Today, I will judge nothing that occurs. I live in the present moment. I let go of hurts and past regrets. My best days are ahead of me. I choose faith instead of fear and worry. I let go of all thoughts that hurt. I am slow to anger. I choose peace over conflict and drama. I focus on the good in all people and all situations. I believe that love never fails. I allow love to be my primary motivation. This is my declaration. Amen!

Daily Declaration #6: Faith in God

I declare that can move mountains. I walk by faith and not my sight. God is fulfilling every good purpose of mine and every act prompted by my faith. A good man out of the good treasure in his heart brings forth that which is good. For as a man thinks in his heart so is he. My words have power and life. My thoughts create my reality. I am a co-creator with God. My words and thoughts cannot return void.

     I use my mind, emotions, and my words to manifest the life I truly desire. I keep my eyes and hope in the Lord. My eyes of understanding are being enlightened. I am filled with Godly wisdom. I trust God beyond what I can see. My eyes are always on God and not my circumstances. I use my faith to cast down doubt and fear. I am more than a conqueror in Christ Jesus who loves me. All things are working together for my highest good. This is my declaration. Amen!

blank
journal
entries

Blank Journal Entries

My Date with God

Date: _____   S   M   T   W   Th   F   S

Activity # 1- Checking In- Today I feel ...

```
┌────────────────────────────────────────────────────┐
│                                                      │
│                                                      │
│                                                      │
│                                                      │
└────────────────────────────────────────────────────┘
```

Activity # 2- My intention for my date with God is ...

```
┌────────────────────────────────────────────────────┐
│                                                      │
│                                                      │
│                                                      │
│                                                      │
└────────────────────────────────────────────────────┘
```

Activity # 3- Meditation

   Title: _____

   Method: _____

                   Today I meditated for _____minutes.

My thoughts during meditation consisted of:

_____
_____
_____

Meditation helped me to release:

_____
_____
_____

After the meditation I felt:

_____
_____
_____

Any additional inspirations or messages from God to you?

```
┌────────────────────────────────────────────────────┐
│                                                      │
│                                                      │
│                                                      │
│                                                      │
└────────────────────────────────────────────────────┘
```

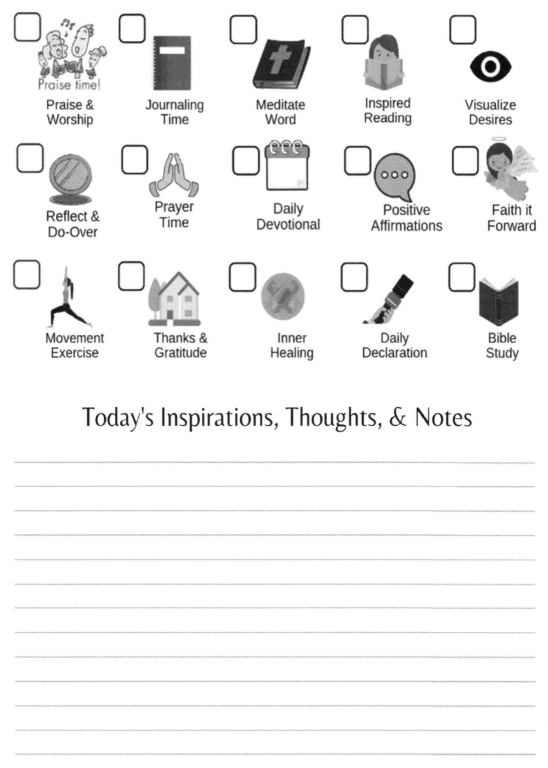

☐ Praise & Worship

☐ Journaling Time

☐ Meditate Word

☐ Inspired Reading

☐ Visualize Desires

☐ Reflect & Do-Over

☐ Prayer Time

☐ Daily Devotional

☐ Positive Affirmations

☐ Faith it Forward

☐ Movement Exercise

☐ Thanks & Gratitude

☐ Inner Healing

☐ Daily Declaration

☐ Bible Study

Today's Inspirations, Thoughts, & Notes

My Date with God

Date: _____   S   M   T   W   Th   F   S

Activity # 1- Checking In- Today I feel ...

Activity # 2- My intention for my date with God is ...

Activity # 3- Meditation

   Title: _____

   Method: _____

                     Today I meditated for _____minutes.

My thoughts during meditation consisted of:

_____
_____
_____

Meditation helped me to release:

_____
_____
_____

After the meditation I felt:

_____
_____
_____

Any additional inspirations or messages from God to you?

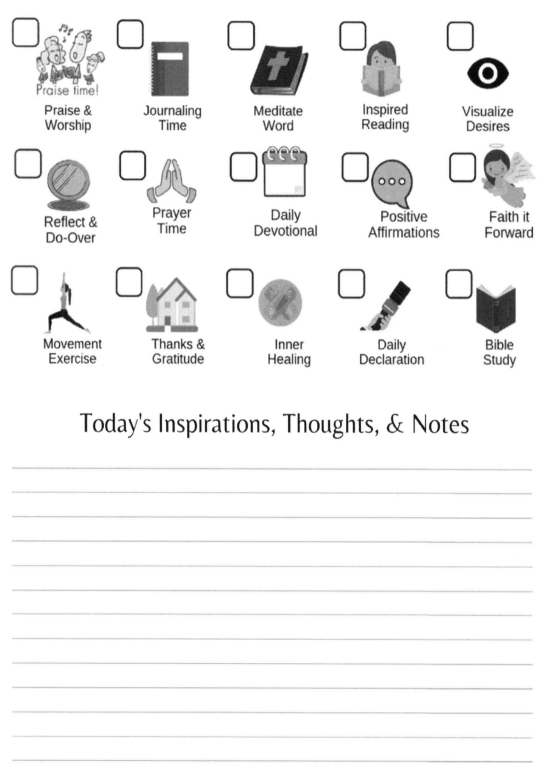

☐ Praise & Worship

☐ Journaling Time

☐ Meditate Word

☐ Inspired Reading

☐ Visualize Desires

☐ Reflect & Do-Over

☐ Prayer Time

☐ Daily Devotional

☐ Positive Affirmations

☐ Faith it Forward

☐ Movement Exercise

☐ Thanks & Gratitude

☐ Inner Healing

☐ Daily Declaration

☐ Bible Study

Today's Inspirations, Thoughts, & Notes

My Date with God

Date: _____   S   M   T   W   Th   F   S

The Basics

Activity # 1- Checking In- Today I feel ...

```



```

Activity # 2- My intention for my date with God is ...

```



```

Activity # 3- Meditation

Title: _____

Method: _____

Today I meditated for _____minutes.

My thoughts during meditation consisted of:

_____
_____
_____

Meditation helped me to release:

_____
_____
_____

After the meditation I felt:

_____
_____
_____

Any additional inspirations or messages from God to you?

```



```

☐ Praise & Worship

☐ Journaling Time

☐ Meditate Word

☐ Inspired Reading

☐ Visualize Desires

☐ Reflect & Do-Over

☐ Prayer Time

☐ Daily Devotional

☐ Positive Affirmations

☐ Faith it Forward

☐ Movement Exercise

☐ Thanks & Gratitude

☐ Inner Healing

☐ Daily Declaration

☐ Bible Study

Today's Inspirations, Thoughts, & Notes

My Date with God

Date: _____

S   M   T   W   Th   F   S

Activity # 1- Checking In- Today I feel ...

Activity # 2- My intention for my date with God is ...

Activity # 3- Meditation

Title: _____

Method: _____

Today I meditated for _____ minutes.

My thoughts during meditation consisted of:

_____
_____
_____

Meditation helped me to release:

_____
_____
_____

After the meditation I felt:

_____
_____
_____

Any additional inspirations or messages from God to you?

Beyond the Basics

☐ Praise & Worship

☐ Journaling Time

☐ Meditate Word

☐ Inspired Reading

☐ Visualize Desires

☐ Reflect & Do-Over

☐ Prayer Time

☐ Daily Devotional

☐ Positive Affirmations

☐ Faith it Forward

☐ Movement Exercise

☐ Thanks & Gratitude

☐ Inner Healing

☐ Daily Declaration

☐ Bible Study

Today's Inspirations, Thoughts, & Notes

My Date with God

Date: _____ S M T W Th F S

Activity # 1- Checking In- Today I feel ...

Activity # 2- My intention for my date with God is ...

Activity # 3- Meditation

Title: _____

Method: _____

Today I meditated for _____minutes.

My thoughts during meditation consisted of:

_____
_____
_____

Meditation helped me to release:

_____
_____
_____

After the meditation I felt:

_____
_____
_____

Any additional inspirations or messages from God to you?

Beyond the Basics

☐ Praise & Worship
☐ Journaling Time
☐ Meditate Word
☐ Inspired Reading
☐ Visualize Desires

☐ Reflect & Do-Over
☐ Prayer Time
☐ Daily Devotional
☐ Positive Affirmations
☐ Faith it Forward

☐ Movement Exercise
☐ Thanks & Gratitude
☐ Inner Healing
☐ Daily Declaration
☐ Bible Study

Today's Inspirations, Thoughts, & Notes

_____

_____

_____

_____

_____

_____

_____

_____

_____

_____

My Date with God

Date: _____   S   M   T   W   Th   F   S

Activity # 1- Checking In- Today I feel ...

```
┌─────────────────────────────────────────────────────┐
│                                                       │
│                                                       │
│                                                       │
│                                                       │
│                                                       │
└─────────────────────────────────────────────────────┘
```

Activity # 2- My intention for my date with God is ...

```
┌─────────────────────────────────────────────────────┐
│                                                       │
│                                                       │
│                                                       │
│                                                       │
└─────────────────────────────────────────────────────┘
```

Activity # 3- Meditation

Title: _____

Method: _____

Today I meditated for _____minutes.

My thoughts during meditation consisted of:

_____
_____
_____

Meditation helped me to release:

_____
_____
_____

After the meditation I felt:

_____
_____
_____

Any additional inspirations or messages from God to you?

```
┌─────────────────────────────────────────────────────┐
│                                                       │
│                                                       │
│                                                       │
│                                                       │
└─────────────────────────────────────────────────────┘
```

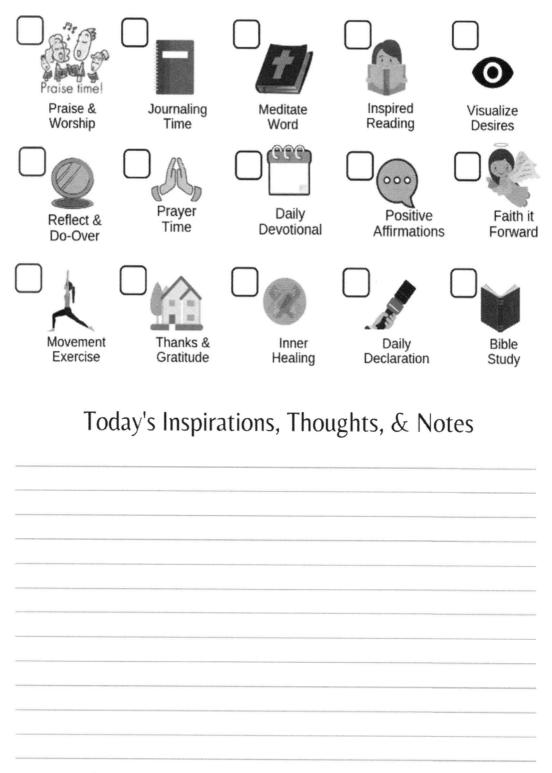

☐ Praise & Worship

☐ Journaling Time

☐ Meditate Word

☐ Inspired Reading

☐ Visualize Desires

☐ Reflect & Do-Over

☐ Prayer Time

☐ Daily Devotional

☐ Positive Affirmations

☐ Faith it Forward

☐ Movement Exercise

☐ Thanks & Gratitude

☐ Inner Healing

☐ Daily Declaration

☐ Bible Study

Today's Inspirations, Thoughts, & Notes

My Date with God

Date: _____   S   M   T   W   Th   F   S

Activity # 1- Checking In- Today I feel ...

Activity # 2- My intention for my date with God is ...

Activity # 3- Meditation

Title: _____

Method: _____

Today I meditated for _____ minutes.

My thoughts during meditation consisted of:

_____
_____
_____

Meditation helped me to release:

_____
_____
_____

After the meditation I felt:

_____
_____
_____

Any additional inspirations or messages from God to you?

☐ Praise & Worship

☐ Journaling Time

☐ Meditate Word

☐ Inspired Reading

☐ Visualize Desires

☐ Reflect & Do-Over

☐ Prayer Time

☐ Daily Devotional

☐ Positive Affirmations

☐ Faith it Forward

☐ Movement Exercise

☐ Thanks & Gratitude

☐ Inner Healing

☐ Daily Declaration

☐ Bible Study

Today's Inspirations, Thoughts, & Notes

My Date with God

Date: _____   S   M   T   W   Th   F   S

Activity # 1- Checking In- Today I feel ...

_____

Activity # 2- My intention for my date with God is ...

_____

Activity # 3- Meditation

Title: _____

Method: _____

Today I meditated for _____ minutes.

My thoughts during meditation consisted of:

_____
_____
_____

Meditation helped me to release:

_____
_____
_____

After the meditation I felt:

_____
_____
_____

Any additional inspirations or messages from God to you?

_____

☐ Praise & Worship

☐ Journaling Time

☐ Meditate Word

☐ Inspired Reading

☐ Visualize Desires

☐ Reflect & Do-Over

☐ Prayer Time

☐ Daily Devotional

☐ Positive Affirmations

☐ Faith it Forward

☐ Movement Exercise

☐ Thanks & Gratitude

☐ Inner Healing

☐ Daily Declaration

☐ Bible Study

Today's Inspirations, Thoughts, & Notes

My Date with God

Date: _____   S   M   T   W   Th   F   S

Activity # 1- Checking In- Today I feel ...

Activity # 2- My intention for my date with God is ...

Activity # 3- Meditation

Title: _____

Method: _____

Today I meditated for _____ minutes.

My thoughts during meditation consisted of:

_____
_____
_____

Meditation helped me to release:

_____
_____
_____

After the meditation I felt:

_____
_____
_____

Any additional inspirations or messages from God to you?

257

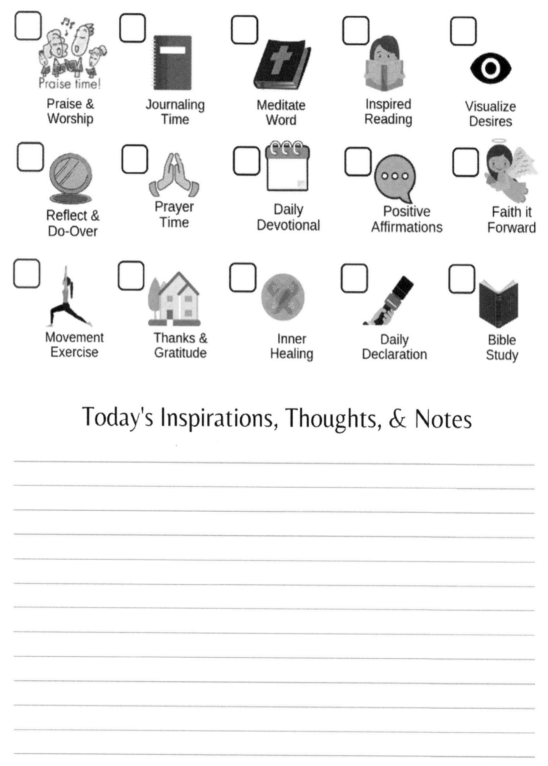

☐ Praise & Worship

☐ Journaling Time

☐ Meditate Word

☐ Inspired Reading

☐ Visualize Desires

☐ Reflect & Do-Over

☐ Prayer Time

☐ Daily Devotional

☐ Positive Affirmations

☐ Faith it Forward

☐ Movement Exercise

☐ Thanks & Gratitude

☐ Inner Healing

☐ Daily Declaration

☐ Bible Study

Today's Inspirations, Thoughts, & Notes

My Date with God

Date: _____   S M T W Th F S

Activity # 1- Checking In- Today I feel ...

Activity # 2- My intention for my date with God is ...

Activity # 3- Meditation

    Title: _____

    Method: _____

            Today I meditated for _____minutes.

My thoughts during meditation consisted of:

_____
_____
_____

Meditation helped me to release:

_____
_____
_____

After the meditation I felt:

_____
_____
_____

Any additional inspirations or messages from God to you?

☐ Praise & Worship
☐ Journaling Time
☐ Meditate Word
☐ Inspired Reading
☐ Visualize Desires

☐ Reflect & Do-Over
☐ Prayer Time
☐ Daily Devotional
☐ Positive Affirmations
☐ Faith it Forward

☐ Movement Exercise
☐ Thanks & Gratitude
☐ Inner Healing
☐ Daily Declaration
☐ Bible Study

Today's Inspirations, Thoughts, & Notes

My Date with God

Date: _____   S   M   T   W   Th   F   S

Activity # 1- Checking In- Today I feel ...

```
┌──────────────────────────────────────────────────┐
│                                                    │
│                                                    │
│                                                    │
│                                                    │
└──────────────────────────────────────────────────┘
```

Activity # 2- My intention for my date with God is ...

```
┌──────────────────────────────────────────────────┐
│                                                    │
│                                                    │
│                                                    │
│                                                    │
└──────────────────────────────────────────────────┘
```

Activity # 3- Meditation

   Title: _____

   Method: _____

                  Today I meditated for _____minutes.

My thoughts during meditation consisted of:

_____
_____
_____

Meditation helped me to release:

_____
_____
_____

After the meditation I felt:

_____
_____
_____

Any additional inspirations or messages from God to you?

```
┌──────────────────────────────────────────────────┐
│                                                    │
│                                                    │
│                                                    │
│                                                    │
└──────────────────────────────────────────────────┘
```

☐ Praise & Worship
☐ Journaling Time
☐ Meditate Word
☐ Inspired Reading
☐ Visualize Desires

☐ Reflect & Do-Over
☐ Prayer Time
☐ Daily Devotional
☐ Positive Affirmations
☐ Faith it Forward

☐ Movement Exercise
☐ Thanks & Gratitude
☐ Inner Healing
☐ Daily Declaration
☐ Bible Study

Today's Inspirations, Thoughts, & Notes

My Date with God

Date: _____   S M T W Th F S

Activity # 1- Checking In- Today I feel ...

```
┌─────────────────────────────────────────────────────────┐
│                                                           │
│                                                           │
│                                                           │
│                                                           │
└─────────────────────────────────────────────────────────┘
```

Activity # 2- My intention for my date with God is ...

```
┌─────────────────────────────────────────────────────────┐
│                                                           │
│                                                           │
│                                                           │
└─────────────────────────────────────────────────────────┘
```

Activity # 3- Meditation

    Title: _____

    Method: _____

          Today I meditated for _____minutes.

My thoughts during meditation consisted of:

_____

_____

_____

Meditation helped me to release:

_____

_____

_____

After the meditation I felt:

_____

_____

_____

Any additional inspirations or messages from God to you?

```
┌─────────────────────────────────────────────────────────┐
│                                                           │
│                                                           │
│                                                           │
│                                                           │
└─────────────────────────────────────────────────────────┘
```

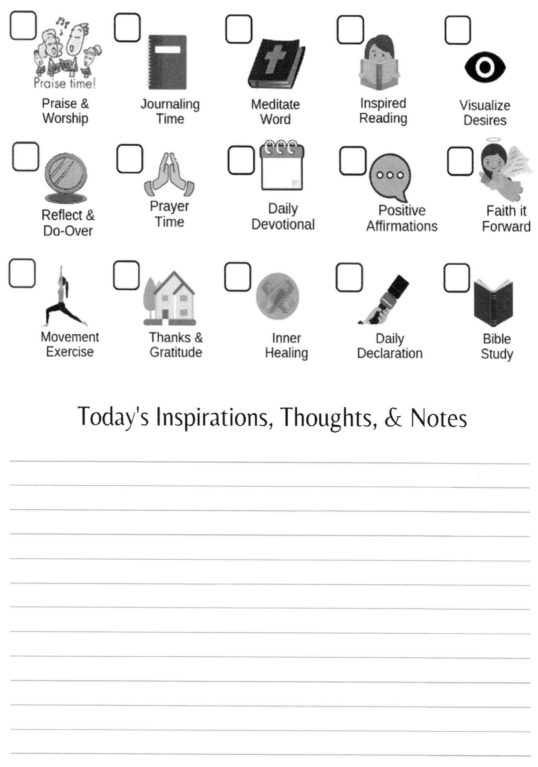

☐ Praise & Worship

☐ Journaling Time

☐ Meditate Word

☐ Inspired Reading

☐ Visualize Desires

☐ Reflect & Do-Over

☐ Prayer Time

☐ Daily Devotional

☐ Positive Affirmations

☐ Faith it Forward

☐ Movement Exercise

☐ Thanks & Gratitude

☐ Inner Healing

☐ Daily Declaration

☐ Bible Study

Today's Inspirations, Thoughts, & Notes

My Date with God

Date: _____   S M T W Th F S

Activity # 1- Checking In- Today I feel ...

Activity # 2- My intention for my date with God is ...

Activity # 3- Meditation

Title: _____

Method: _____

Today I meditated for _____minutes.

My thoughts during meditation consisted of:

_____
_____
_____

Meditation helped me to release:

_____
_____
_____

After the meditation I felt:

_____
_____
_____

Any additional inspirations or messages from God to you?

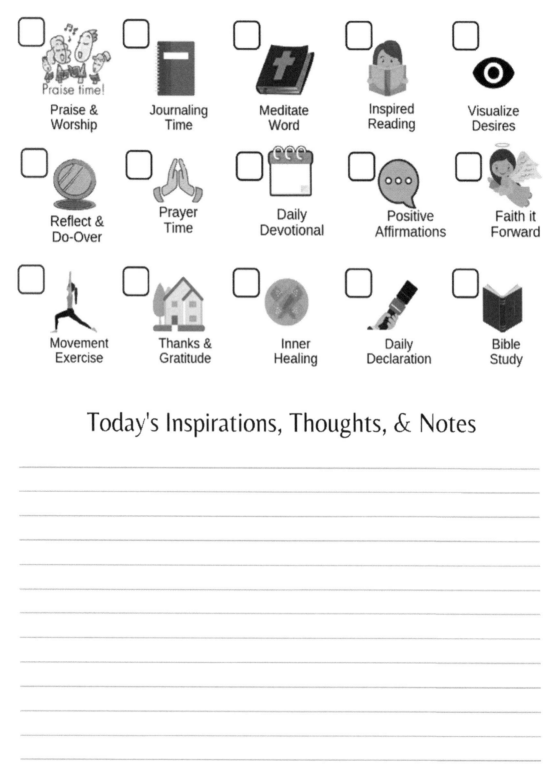

☐ Praise & Worship

☐ Journaling Time

☐ Meditate Word

☐ Inspired Reading

☐ Visualize Desires

☐ Reflect & Do-Over

☐ Prayer Time

☐ Daily Devotional

☐ Positive Affirmations

☐ Faith it Forward

☐ Movement Exercise

☐ Thanks & Gratitude

☐ Inner Healing

☐ Daily Declaration

☐ Bible Study

Today's Inspirations, Thoughts, & Notes

About the Author

Rhonda Jones is the creator of the award-winning website, The Christian Meditator, and the creator of over 23 Christ-centered meditation and affirmations CDs on a variety of topics. Rhonda's meditations allow Christians to meditate in a way that completely honors God and will not conflict with their Christian faith. Coming soon are her new books, *Detox Your Life & Awaken Your Inner Spirit, and the Design Your Day, Design Your Life Journal. Detox Your Life & Awaken Your Inner Spirit* is a 12-week Biblically based program that integrates Christian Meditation and God's Word with spiritual and practical lessons to help believers find healing and balance in seven core areas of their lives. Rhonda facilitates yearly God Getaway Retreats to help believers create or deepen their Christian meditation practice. Contact Rhonda via email at thechristianmeditator@yahoo.com.

Need a Speaker

Need a speaker for your group, event, or church community? See Rhonda's speaker page at **Christian Women Speakers** at:

https://www.womenspeakers.com/united-states/sacramento/speaker/rhonda-jones

Personal Christian Meditation & Healing Group Mini-Retreats

Interested in hosting a mini-personal retreat for your group of 8-10, contact Rhonda at thechristianmeditator@yahoo.com to receive more information.

Host a Christian Meditation Class or Group

Want to host your own Christian meditation class or group using The Christian Meditation Journal, you can get free access to my *Leader's Guide*.

Bulk Paperback Book Copies Available

Interested in buying 10 or more copies, please send an email to receive our discounted bulk pricing information.

Coming in 2019 and 2020:

Design Your Day, Design Your Life Manifesting Journal

Detox Your Life and Awaken Your Inner Spirit.

More Books by Rhonda

Unplug Christian Meditation Personal Retreat Kit

Renew Your Mind Christian Meditation Course

No Prep Christian Yoga Plans (For Faith-based yoga teachers)

Rhonda's Online Course:

Introduction to Christian Meditation with Rhonda Jones

Abiding in Christ Christian Meditation Course

God Getaway Retreats

Join Rhonda for a God Getaways Retreats. Learn more at https://godgetaways.com

Join the Christian Meditator Mailing Lists!

https://thechristianmeditator.com

https://thechristianmeditationjournal.com

https://godgetaways.com

Need additional blank journal entries?

Visit:
https://christianmeditationjournal.com
and order a book of journal entries only.

Please Send Your Feedback!

If you enjoyed the *Christian Meditation Journal*, please **leave an Amazon testimonial** and email me a copy at thechristianmeditator@yahoo.com

More at TheChristianMeditator.com